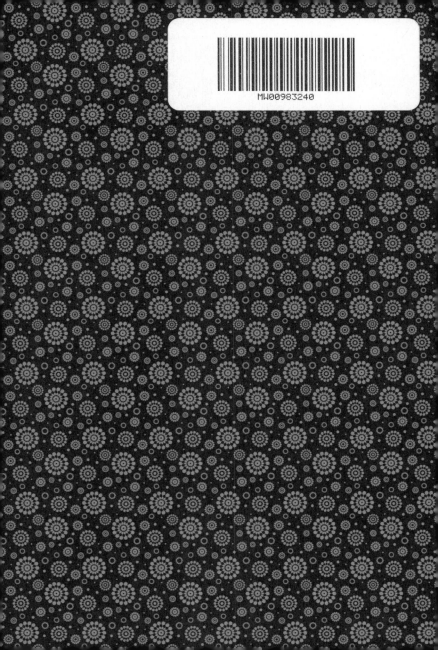

"*They Call Me Mom* is spit-out-your-coffee hysterical and equally poignant. Michelle and Bethany hold nothing back in these highly relatable devotions about their lives as mothers. Full of God's love and encouragement, this book is one you'll binge read in between making peanut butter and jelly sandwiches for your kids—it's that addicting!"

SARAH PHILPOTT, PhD, farm mama of three, award-winning author of *Loved Baby*, and blogger at allamericanmom.net

"If you're a mom looking for wisdom, advice, and spiritual support, read this book. With gut-level honesty and laugh-out-loud humor, Michelle Medlock Adams and Bethany Jett reveal their own teachable moments and insights from the best and worst days of motherhood. This is a book you'll want to give to every mom you know!"

CAROL KENT, speaker and author of *He Holds My Hand*

"A beautiful and thoughtful devotional from Michelle Medlock Adams and Bethany Jett, bathed in spiritual truths yet honest that even one of God's greatest gifts to women has its difficult moments. Highly recommended for all moms who recognize this incredible motherhood thing is full of joy and sadness, peace and chaos, successes and, well, the other stuff. This devotional reminds us that all these are the plans of our Savior, and they are all for our good. Oh, and if you're the 'perfect' mom, this might not be the devotional for you!"

MICHELLE TESORI, cofounder of the Tesori Family Foundation

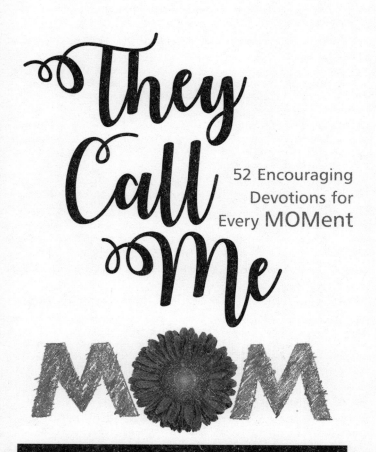

They Call Me

52 Encouraging Devotions for Every MOMent

Me

MOM

MICHELLE MEDLOCK ADAMS and BETHANY JETT

Kregel
Publications

Chapters 18 and 32 are based on content first published by Guideposts, a Church Corp. Used with permission.

Published in association with Cyle Young of the Hartline Literary Agency, LLC.

ISBN 978-0-8254-4616-0, print
ISBN 978-0-8254-7591-7, epub

Printed in the United States of America
19 20 21 22 23 24 25 26 27 28 / 5 4 3 2 1

For my precious daughters,

Abby Leigh and Allyson Michelle:

I'm so honored that you call me Mom and I'm so excited

that you two are now experiencing this amazing thing

called motherhood.

Love you more!

To Jeremiah, Jedidiah, and Josiah:

You are the three best gifts a mom could ever wish for.

I love you millions and millions and more.

Contents

Introduction

"**Mom**" is the best title we'll ever have the honor of holding, yet it's also one of the hardest jobs we'll ever have the pleasure of doing. That's why we need our #momtribe to support us, pray for us, and cheer us on as we care for those precious gifts from God.

It was our greatest desire to be real—no pretenses—in this book, because being a mom means we're real, sometimes raw, and usually running on caffeine.

We hope you'll enjoy a good laugh as we share our crazy, idiotic mom moments, relate to our biggest mommy fails and challenges, and be inspired to run this mommy race with a bit more pep in your step.

Within these pages, you'll find inspirational messages with Scripture verses and applications, as well as sidebars featuring practical, helpful information. We hope you find it all useful.

It's our goal that you feel supported, encouraged, and loved as you read each entry, because we are in your corner and we prayed over this book from the planning stages to the moment we hit Send on this manuscript.

Lastly, remember: they call you Mom, but God calls you chosen, empowered, treasured, and more than enough.

And us? We call you friend. Hugs!

1

They Call Me Dream Chaser

Bethany's JETTliner

*T*he *Greatest Showman* soundtrack gets my pulse racing and my blood pumping. When little P. T. Barnum sings "A Million Dreams," I feel the words soar through my soul, and when I look at my kids, I see that same starry-eyed look reflected in their faces.

The look of a dream chaser.

What dream do you chase?

Does your heart stretch out its fingertips to grasp the elusive tail end of a fantasy so big that it doesn't seem like reality could ever be possible?

Do you ever read a book or watch a show and resonate strongly with a character because you want to be her or wish you knew the things she did? Have you ever wondered what your life would be like if you'd taken a different path?

Sometimes you don't know what your dreams are, and sometimes there's a tiny niggle in your heart—an unspoken unrest—when you just know that you're meant for greater things. You were meant to make a difference.

Sometimes it's fear of failure that keeps us from stepping out of our comfort zones.

In Ephesians 4:1 Paul begs that we live a life worthy of our calling, because we *have* been called. Indeed, God has a purpose for our lives. Granted, that purpose is not always revealed right away. Sometimes we are in the training-pants part of our journey while we prepare for our big-girl panties.

Sometimes we don't always follow the path God laid out for us. However, our loving Father always provides a way for us to return. We can open our arms and catch the vision and purpose God has set.

If you ask my kids right now what they want to do when they grow up, all three of them will say the same thing: "I want to be a YouTuber." And I say, "Baby, you can definitely be a YouTuber." In fact, many You-Tubers make a ton more money than we do. If they can support themselves, help others, and honor God, then babies, go be YouTubers.

It's important that our kids walk through the dream-chasing process with us. When I have a business meeting that I'm nervous about, I ask my boys to pray for the call. We'll jump up and down together if the call went well. When a book contract comes in, we pile in the car and head out for frozen yogurt covered in fruit, candy, and syrupy goodness.

They see the hustle and they witness the heartache. Owning a business means putting out fires along with storing up wins. Our kids need to see that not everything goes right all the time. The example we set instills the confidence and coping skills they'll need as adults when they face these same types of issues.

Not everyone is nice. Not every dream pans out.

The key is to know that you've got God on your side and when you confidently walk in His plan, those missteps and hardships are redeemed in His timing.

God's purpose for us and our natural inclination and talents work hand in hand. We encourage our kids to chase their dreams by encouraging them to share with us their passions.

It's not our job to squash their dreams but to guide them into following the call God has on their lives. I don't know God's plan for each one of them, but I know my job is to help water the seeds that God has planted in their hearts. When they are old enough to make decisions for themselves, I'll be right there to guide them as I pray for them.

And when we turn the volume high and belt out "A Million Dreams" together, the look on their faces matches the song of my heart, and I dream.

Michelle's Intel

Whenever I speak about being a writer at Young Authors Day programs, I always take time to ask the students what they want to be when they grow up.

You know what I've discovered?

Little bitty kids can have great big dreams. Some children answer "firefighter," "nurse," "teacher," "writer," "artist," "policeman," or "movie star." Still others say "model," "race car driver," "professional baseball player," "scientist," "president," and so many more awesome occupations.

Bottom line—children know how to dream big.

Do you know why? Because no one has told them yet that they can't dream big, and they don't have that inner dialogue that says, "You can't be a movie star. You're not pretty enough. You'll never be able to accomplish your dream." They truly believe they can do anything. And you know what? They're right!

Encourage your children to dream big, and then follow their example.

We should all be able to believe *big* when it comes to the dreams and ambitions that God has placed within us. Our heavenly Father wouldn't have placed them there if He weren't going to help us achieve them. So, encourage your little dreamers, and use your childlike faith to start believing *big*.

God Calls Me Dreamer

The Bible says that God will give us the desire of our heart (Ps. 37:4), but it's important that we also pray for God to align our hearts with His. We don't want to chase the dreams of our own making, but the dreams that God gives us. Psalm 32:8 says, "I will instruct you and teach you in the way you should go; I will counsel you with my loving eye on you." Our prayer should be for our children to pursue God's will and for God to equip us with wisdom to help guide their paths.

How to Create Vision Boards

Vision boards are creative expressions of our goals and passions . . . and they're an inexpensive and relatively nonmessy activity! Supplies needed: construction paper, poster board, magazines, glue, scissors, and any fun crafty extras you have on hand. This is something you can do right alongside your kids.

Step one: Brainstorm with your kiddos, discussing wishes, dreams, and goals that could be the inspiration for your individual boards. (By the way, you can have more than one board. For example, I have a health and fitness vision board and a family vision board.)

Step two: Pull or cut out anything from the magazine that conveys the goal or want. It can be pictures or words.

Step three: Space the cutouts in a pleasing way on the poster board.

Step four: Glue the pieces in place.

Step five: Hang the poster somewhere it can remind you and your children of your goals.

Voilà! Your very own vision board. As a bonus, have your children share why they chose the words and pictures they did and what those things mean to them. Lastly, be sure to hang on to those vision boards for nostalgia's sake and so you can celebrate together when those goals and dreams are accomplished.

2

They Call Me Loving (No Matter What)

Michelle's Intel

I already had one beautiful baby girl, Abby Leigh, and as I watched baby number two on the ultrasound screen, I couldn't help but secretly hope for another girl. I loved the Laura Ashley nursery at our little house. I loved all the pink outfits, the ruffles, the bows, the sparkly shoes. I loved it all! But I also knew I'd love a baby boy just as much, and I was well aware that a boy would make Jeff's mom happy since he would carry on the Adams name. With Jeff being an only child, that duty fell on us.

"Let's see if your baby is going to cooperate today," the nurse whispered in the dimly lit examination room.

Jeff squeezed my hand. I smiled up at him, so excited to learn the sex of baby number two.

It seemed like the nurse moved the wand up and down and across my petroleum-jellied belly for an hour.

"Oh, there it is. I can confidently tell you the sex of your baby," she said, printing out a few pictures. "Are you sure you want to know?"

"Yes," we said in unison.

"You're having another little girl! Congratulations!"

Jeff kissed my hand he was already holding, and I cried tears of joy. I was so happy I was having another baby girl, a little sister for Abby.

Jeff's mom also cried when she heard the news—I'm not sure her tears were ones of joy because she really wanted a boy, but what she didn't know at that moment was how close she and Allyson would become. Best friends.

On the drive home from the doctor's office that day, I worried Jeff might be disappointed we weren't having a boy, but even before I could voice my concerns, he said, "I'm so glad we're having another girl. They are so precious."

And boy, do they love their daddy. There's truth behind that song, "Daddy's Little Girl," for sure!

Life with girls has been such a blessing; okay, not every day but most days. If you're a #momofgirls you're nodding your head right now. Being a mom of two amazing daughters is great in many ways—we share shoes, clothes, makeup, and a love for romantic comedies. It's been great to see my girls excel in gymnastics and cheerleading since those were sports I also enjoyed when I was growing up. And I've loved being able to give them advice about dating, frenemies, and "girl stuff" over the years.

I've also enjoyed sharing some not-so-girly passions with them—Cubs baseball and bass fishing. Yes, we're a Cubbies-loving, bass-fishing family, and we wouldn't have it any other way.

Now, listen. Raising girls hasn't been all butterflies and sunshine and bluebirds sitting on my shoulders. We've had screaming matches. We've had seasons when Abby wanted to move out because I was, and I quote, "the worst mother in the world." And we've battled some serious health issues with Allyson. It wasn't always easy, but it was always worth it.

So many times, I've fallen on my face before God and asked for His intervention—that He would help me parent my girls—because many days I felt like I was falling short. I wondered if I was good enough, smart enough, strong enough, or simply enough. I found out that I wasn't, but He was, and with God's help, I can testify from the other side—we made it!

Both Abby and Ally have grown into remarkable young women. Both love Jesus. Both graduated college and are excelling in their respective careers. And both are happily married and starting families. Jeff and I stand in awe of our daughters.

I wish I could take credit for any of it, but honestly, I can't.

It's all Jesus.

I don't know what stage you're in these days, but wherever you are on this motherhood journey, just know you're not alone. Include God in every stage, at every age. Let Him direct your steps, as it says in Proverbs, and trust Him in the big and little decisions. Whether you're a #boymom or a #girlmom, it doesn't matter because you're a loved #childofGod, and with your heavenly Father by your side, you're going to rock this!

Bethany's JETTliner

I was thrilled when I found out I was pregnant with baby number one. It didn't matter if I was having a boy or a girl. But apparently my husband had secret hopes for a boy—his face when the ultrasound technician pointed out our son on the monitor was priceless. I prayed for a girl with baby number two, but once again we saw male baby bits on the monitor. I teared up but found solace that my sons would have each other and would be best friends.

When God blessed us with baby number three, I prayed hard for a girl. I knew this might be my last opportunity to be pregnant, so I asked God for the desire of my heart.

When baby number three revealed himself at the ultrasound, I cried. Then I felt guilty for crying. My baby was healthy, and he was a blessing.

I'll never know what a little mini-me would look like or be able to raise a godly daughter. However, I have the privilege to raise three amazing little boys into godly men.

My boys know that at one time I'd wished for a girl, but they know this truth: God told me *no* because He has a special plan for each one of their lives. He wanted Jeremy, Jedidiah, and Josiah to be each other's brothers, and God wanted my husband and me to raise them to love Him and one another.

I take this responsibility extremely seriously. The Bible says that God knit every single one of my crazy, rambunctious children together in my womb. I've grown into my role as a boy-mama, and I cherish every dirt-filled mischievous moment. I may have had a different original plan, but my boys are exactly what God knew I needed.

God Calls Me His Child

John 1:12 says, "But to all who believed him and accepted him, he gave the right to become children of God" (NLT). Isn't that amazing? I know that's a title we throw around a lot in Christian circles, but when you realize that you're a child of God—that's life-changing. If God had a hashtag, it would be #FatherofAll followed by #HeAdoresUs—how great is that? He loved us before we were even born, and though we can be a handful (like our own children), He still adores us, believes in us, and is proud of us. Think how much you love your kiddos (regardless of whether they wear tiaras or dirt). Well, God loves us even more! That changes everything.

Five #MomofGirls Quotes

- "A mother's treasure is her daughter."

- "A daughter is someone you laugh with, dream with, and love with all your heart."

- "A daughter is just a little girl who grows up to be your best friend."

- "Happiness is mother-daughter time."

- "A daughter is God's way of saying, 'Thought you could use a life-long friend.'"

3

They Call Me Calm in the Chaos

Bethany's JETTliner

Raising boys is not for the faint of heart.

Honestly, I have never paid so much attention to the state of the bathroom as I have after my boys outgrew their diapers. I don't know why I'm ever shocked to find spit wads above the shower or pee in the tub.

I'll think, "Haven't I raised them better than this?" and then I remember this simple truth: I'm not done raising them yet. It's my job to continue to say the words, "Stop throwing toilet paper on the ceiling," and "Pee-pee goes in the potty, nowhere else."

Raising a son means that we have to learn, understand, and accept the innate personalities, character, and temperament that comes with that Y chromosome. My husband understands our boys in ways that I never will, but I believe that it's our job as #boymoms to raise sons who understand women and respect our differences. It's our job to protect them, cherish them, and fight for their rights to be boys in an ever-growing male-bashing society.

This can be difficult, especially when the behavior is so far from what you would ever do yourself.

For example, I've never felt compelled to pick my nose and wipe the contents on my wall, but recently my son left bloodstains on my white bedspread because he wouldn't stop picking a scab.

Thankfully, a little Spray 'n Wash and everything was as good as new.

My sister Jill has two little girls and when we're blessed to all be together, it's interesting to watch the dynamics of the children. My nieces will sit and color quietly for hours. She can let them use paint and Play-Doh without worry. The girls will dress their Barbies and make up stories for them, while my boys find ways to catapult them.

A marker in my niece's hands is a creative outlet to express herself.

In my son's, it's a sword, a tattoo-creator, and self-given permission to draw on his brother.

Jill can't handle all the running in my house, which to me is simply what I call "boy-mode fast walking," and I can't concentrate with the higher-pitched shrieks and giggles that emit from my beautiful nieces. I will admit that I get a kick out of watching the girls react to each other. There are little headshakes, attitudes, and drama that are absent from my house, yet I'm used to the boys wrestling, yelling, or trying to throw a punch if I'm not looking.

My mom has remarked even watching us parent is different. My sister uses a calmer tone and more dialogue with her daughters, whereas I go straight to the bottom line with the boys and use a firmer tone of voice.

And yet, despite my boys' obsession with bathroom humor (although I know girls do this too) and constant need to antagonize one another, boys have a way of burrowing their dirt-streaked little faces into your shoulder and making you feel like the most amazing person in the whole world.

Truly, though, I think being a boy mom is hard these days. Our society is obsessed with crossing gender lines and it's almost taboo to "be a real man." The biblical example is taught as archaic, and strong male role models are hard to come by. We're in the day and age of girls not needing to be rescued by a man. While I'm an advocate of strong women and independence, I also believe that strong women know how to respect the unique inner workings of men. Sadly, masculinity is being squashed and it's my fear that the wrong lips will whisper lies into my sons' ears and that they'll believe they're "less than" because they are male.

Boys have a hero complex. There is an innate desire to "mommy-please," which differs from people-pleasing because boys want to please their mommies and daddies in different ways. As moms, we must over-communicate our boys' positive behavior because we live in an overly critical society. We are the ones who have to instill the positivity.

When they pick you a pretty weed, it's got to be the most precious flower you've ever seen. When they open a door or show kindness, we need to praise them.

I've seen firsthand the damage a mother can do by rejecting those small acts of kindness. A friend of ours has a hard time giving his wife, whom he loves fiercely, gifts of any kind. It stresses him in a strange way. When his wife finally got to the root of that anxiety, she was stunned. As a child, his elementary class rewarded the students with "school bucks" to shop from their little store. The items were all cheap plastic toys, but our friend worked for those school bucks so he could get his mom a birthday present.

When he presented her with the gift, she said, "Why did you waste your money on this?"

Oh no.

No . . . no . . . no . . .

That rejection manifested into a subconscious fear to give gifts in the future. My friend hadn't even realized that this one moment from his childhood affected him so strongly until his wife got him to open up.

Additionally, it's our job to teach our sons how to respect women. When we teach our boys to respect the words we say—and the "mom look" when words aren't needed—we're teaching them to respect the women who will be their bosses, business partners, and authority figures.

When we teach them to honor women with "ladies first" and using "ma'am" at the appropriate time, we're teaching them to put others first, particularly women, so that one day they will respect their wives.

When we teach them to do household chores like laundry, dishes, and vacuuming, we're teaching them to be self-sufficient and providing a model that I hope they carry into adulthood.

When we lead by example, by pursuing our goals, chasing our dreams, and working hard, we teach them to respect women as their partners and equals.

We teach them to honor women as Jesus did.

I may not have daughters to raise as strong, fierce women of God, but I have sons who will respect the daughters of the women who do.

Michelle's Intel

I never had any little boys to raise, though I think I would have enjoyed that adventure. No, I'm #girlmom all the way. Hair bows. Lip gloss. Glittery nail polish. Barbie dolls. Tutus. And shiny shoes. That's what little girls are made of . . . but not all little girls.

Though my daughters are only twenty months apart, have the same two parents, and were raised the very same way, they could not be more different. From the very beginning, my daughters had distinct personalities and preferences.

For example, I could get Abby ready for church and she would still look picture-perfect at bedtime, with her hair bow still in place. Now, Ally was a whole different story. By the time we arrived at church, just ten minutes from the house, she would have a dirty face, ripped tights, and a missing hair bow. And on occasion we'd learn from the nursery worker that Ally had also lost her potty pants somewhere along the way. #truestory

Abby hated getting dirty, while Ally lived for it!

Abby was grossed out by worms, bugs, and lizards.

Ally loved to catch lizards and actually had a pet lizard that she fed crickets!

And the list goes on and on.

We learned early in this parenting gig that not all little girls are the same, and that's okay. In fact, that's more than okay; it's amazing. Just think how boring life would be if we were all the same.

Knowing that, Jeff and I were careful to celebrate their individual strengths and appreciate their differences so we wouldn't squelch their little spirits. We encouraged them to follow their passions, redirected them if they lost their way, and cheered them on in every endeavor.

As different as they were, our girls had several important things in common. They loved their friends and family. They loved Jesus. And they loved each other. With those common denominators, we knew we were doing something right, and we praised God for helping us parent our daughters.

We always teased that Ally was the boy we never had, and then she grew up into this feminine, petite, makeup-wearing Barbie doll who went to fashion school.

You just never know what God has planned.

So, whether you're a #boymom, #girlmom, or #momofboth, make sure you encourage your kiddos to think outside the box, follow their dreams, and become the world-changers that God made them to be.

God Calls Me Equipped

Mary was the original boy mama. Her relationship with Jesus was unlike any that we'll ever know this side of heaven. She literally raised the perfect son. I can't imagine the pressure she must have felt at times. Mary was the chosen one, the only woman in the whole world that God deemed worthy to raise His Son. And even though she had no experience raising boys (or any kids, for that matter!), God equipped her and we can trust that He will equip us too. Hebrews 13:21 says that He will "equip you with everything good that you may do his will, working in us that which is pleasing in his sight, through Jesus Christ, to whom be glory forever and ever. Amen" (ESV).

How to Thrive with Little Boys

- Give good-morning hugs.
- Let them run off their energy.
- Play with them.
- Read out loud.
- Encourage them to verbalize their feelings.
- Keep plenty of healthy snacks on hand.
- Teach them positive touch associations by putting your hand on their shoulder or arm when talking to them.
- Be prepared for messes and bathroom humor.
- Invest in wet wipes.
- Always kiss them goodnight.

4

They Call Me Mean Mommy

Michelle's Intel

What could be better than a handmade, beautifully colored Mother's Day card from your child?

Eight-year-old Abby handed me the card she'd made especially for me. It was lovely, with a bright purple flower on the front and the words, "Best Mommy Ever!" written in pink crayon on the inside. I hugged Ab and thanked her for her thoughtfulness. She smiled and skipped away but not before handing me a box of Junior Mints—my fave. It was shaping up to be a pretty amazing Mother's Day.

Seven-year-old Allyson was putting the finishing touches on her card while I put the roses Jeff had given me in some water.

"Okay, I'm all done," Ally said, handing me her masterpiece. The cover of the card was decorated with a beautiful rainbow and several gold star stickers surrounding the words "Happy Mother's Day, Mommy!" I smiled and opened the card to see what other sweet drawings and messages my younger daughter had created just for me. I read the words inside several times to make sure I was reading what I thought I was reading.

There it was, in bright blue crayon, my special Mother's Day message: "Mom, you're not mean all the time. Love, Ally."

Bet you can't buy that card in Hallmark!

One thing is for sure: it was definitely heartfelt. I knew Ally wasn't trying to hurt my feelings, but honesty hurts sometimes, doesn't it? And kids, especially when they're *your* kids, are brutally honest.

I'm not sure what prompted Ally to write those sentiments that particular Mother's Day, and she can't remember either because I've asked her. But no matter what motivated her message, it certainly communicated volumes to me. I laughed it off when I shared the card with my husband, but inside I was dying. I wondered if my girls would always think of me as a "mean mommy." I didn't want to be Mean Mommy, but it seemed my lot in life since I was more of the disciplinarian and Jeff was more of the "fun parent."

That night when I went to bed, my mind was racing with every "mommy fail" moment I'd ever had. Of course, I didn't consider any of the good things I'd done. No, I could only think of the times I'd messed up. Ever been there?

The devil is happy to point out all our failures, and if we meditate on them too long, it can take us to a very dark place. The Bible says we're all attaining from glory to glory (2 Cor. 3:18). In other words, we're not perfect and that's okay because He is perfect, and He has our backs.

I heard a story recently about a woman who was thinking about all the bad things she'd done in her life and all the poor decisions she'd made. Later that night, she had a vivid dream. She was in a large room with dozens of filing cabinets, and inside those filing cabinets were note cards filled with every action she'd ever taken in her life—the good, the bad, and the ugly. Panicking, she tried desperately to erase her failures from the note cards, but they wouldn't erase. She tried harder. Still, they wouldn't budge. Just then, Jesus walked into the room, and she thought, "Oh great. I don't want to see Him right now. I don't want Him to know about all the times I've messed up." Jesus looked at her, and just as she was about to cower down in front of Him, so ashamed over her mistakes, He took out a red pen and started writing, "Paid in Full" on every note card.

That's how we need to see all of our "mommy fails" in life—they have been paid in full. God adores us even when we forget to take cookies to the holiday party at school. He still loves us when we lose our patience and snap at our children. He still loves us when we order pizza for the third night in a row because we're too tired to get to the grocery store. Should we do better? Yes. But His love for us isn't based on our performance. He loves us unconditionally.

And here's more good news. Your children may call you "mean mommy" from time to time. They may even scream, "You're ruining my life," during their teen years. But they don't mean those things. They love you. They need you. And you'll always be their mommy—mean or not. Just remember, the next time you have a "mommy fail" kind of day, your mistake has already been paid in full.

Bethany's JETTliner

Someone told me once (barring any actual cruelty) that if your kids think you're mean, it means you're doing something right. My boys definitely think I'm mean when I take away their video games or ground them from screens. I asked my youngest if I've ever been mean to him, and he said, "You're not mean, but you've hurt my feelings."

What! Nooooo!

I never want to hurt my kids' feelings, and it breaks my heart that

I have. The beautiful thing about having a relationship with your kids is the ability to be honest and ask for forgiveness when we mess up. Because we're going to mess up and sometimes we do hurt our children's feelings.

I told my son to let me know if I hurt his feelings again in the future. I know that as my boys grow into teenagers there will be plenty of opportunities when I'll have to put my foot down and enforce rules that my boys won't like. I know my "mean mommy" days are coming, but I hope to keep an open line of communication with them so we can get through those days together.

God Calls Me Forgiven

First John 1:9 assures us, "If we confess our sins, he is faithful and just to forgive us our sins and to cleanse us from all unrighteousness" (ESV). In other words, we are forgiven. Our heavenly Father isn't mad at us; He is madly in love with us. All we have to do is trust Him with our lives and our children, and live like we're forgiven. Hold your head up, sister. Your debt has been paid in full!

On Those Mean Mommy Days . . .

If your tween daughter just yelled, "I hate you!" as she slammed her bedroom door, don't freak out. As hurtful as this is, it's pretty normal, and you'll probably hear it again before she graduates from high school. You have to think of this "I hate you" as just a bad "I love you" day because, in reality, that's all it is. Try not to take it personally and carry on being Mom. Don't be guilted into any other role, because while we want to be friends with our children, it's not a very effective way to parent.

In the article, "Why You Can't Be Your Child's Friend," on empowering parents.com, the parenting expert writes: "Our role as parents is really to teach, coach and give our kids consequences when they misbehave. If you slip into that friend role, however, it's virtually impossible to lay down the law and set limits on your child's inappropriate behavior."[1]

Resist the urge to be your daughter's bestie or your son's buddy, and keep being Mommy. They have enough friends, but they only have one you!

1. Janet Lehman, "Why You Can't Be Your Child's Friend," Empowering Parents, accessed August 2, 2019, https://www.empoweringparents.com/article/why-you-cant-be-your-childs-friend/.

5

They Call Me Teacher

Bethany's JETTliner

There are times I look at my children and think, "Where are your parents?"

When my son tells a lie, hits his sibling, or destroys his brother's Minecraft house that took three hours to create, I want to say, "Don't you know better? Haven't I raised you better than this?"

But the answer that comes to my spirit is, "Not yet."

I'm the one who has to raise them. Train them. Guide them. Teach them. I'm the one who corrects the disobedience so one day when they become adults, they'll have learned self-control and be productive citizens.

This is the reminder I told myself when, after taking ten minutes to be alone, I came downstairs to find French onion dip on the wall and taco meat scattered on the tile floor like confetti on New Year's.

Did I mention I was homeschooling all three of them while my husband was on a six-month military deployment?

Sometimes there are no words.

It's moments like this when we take a deep breath and pray to the Almighty God for strength and patience and peace before we go all Madea on them.

My boys are still learning. And I'm learning with them.

This teaching begins the moment our kids are born. We immediately try to get our infants on a schedule, although the first few weeks are usually dictated by the newcomer in the footie onesie.

We coo our names to them. "Ma-ma. Da-da."

We show them every object we can find in singsong high-pitched voices. "There's a puppy! See the horsey? Pet the kitty." *Apparently, the objects are restricted to animals.*

We teach them by example, as well.

It's amazing how many times strange phrases will pop out of my sons' mouths. They are always listening. Observing. Learning.

It's a little scary sometimes how well-tuned our children are when we're speaking to other adults and move from normal to hushed tones. My husband, Justin, and I used to spell out words when the boys were little. Then one day our kindergartner said from the back seat, "I know you're spelling the words *ice cream* and I want some."

After listening to a talk radio segment on parenting, Justin and I more fully understood how our behaviors affected our children. The show discussed how risky parental behaviors increase the likelihood that children will adopt those same behaviors. It makes sense that if a parent smokes, their child may smoke too. However, it seems "that adolescents whose parents smoke, drink, or drive without seat belts are especially likely to engage in early and unsafe sexual activity."[2] Who knew?

2. Esther I. Wilder and Toni Terling Watt, "Risky Parental Behavior and Adolescent Sexual Activity at First Coitus," *Milbank Quarterly* 80, no. 3 (September 2002): 481–524, https://www.ncbi.nlm.nih.gov/pubmed/12233247.

Not only do our kids watch what we do, they watch what we *don't* do, like not wearing a seat belt while driving. This awareness has led us to become more cautious in what we do and don't do in the Jett house (and the Jett car!). We develop "house rules," and it's always interesting to hear from other families what their "house rules" are, like "no food in the bedrooms . . . or anyone of the opposite sex *ever*."

The house rules became even more heightened when we chose to pull our littles from the school system. We wanted to create some stability since we were moving twice within a six-month time frame for the military.

Home economics became part of our curriculum, and the boys got to witness my sometimes frantic balancing act of teaching them, building a business, and trying with all my might to keep clean a house where four people spend the majority of their time.

Proverbs 22:6 says if we start children on the way they should go, they will not depart, and there are a lot of interesting takes on this verse. I believe the verse means that we not only have to look to the general way all children should go, but we also need to be aware of the individual paths each of our kids should take. That means parenting in a different way for each one.

I believe it means taking into account their unique personalities and nurturing the gifts that God has given them. I also believe it means disciplining each child the way they need to be disciplined. My extremely introverted son doesn't mind a time-out, yet time-out and groundings work really well for my son whose primary love language is quality time.

So, when there's French onion dip on the wall, taco-seasoned ground turkey on the tile, and you're ready to pull out your messy-bunned hair in frustration, remember that you're not alone. Take a deep breath, pray a prayer of strength, pass out paper towels and Clorox wipes, and go sit on the couch and dream up a suitable punishment while your sweet babies clean up their mess.

And P.S. Everyone wears a seat belt, no matter what!

Michelle's Intel

I don't know who first coined the phrase "teachable moments" but those two words are both a blessing and a curse. When we are purposely trying to impart words of wisdom through a teachable moment, it's a good thing. But when we accidentally have a "teachable moment" we didn't intend, and our kiddos grab on to our bad behavior, it's not so wonderful.

Here's the good news. Even when we miss it and we have a not-so-lovely teachable moment, God gives us grace. (He doesn't expect us to be perfect moms. He knows all our flaws and yet He still adores us.) And you know what else? Sometimes it's an even more powerful teachable moment when we get it wrong and have the courage to admit, "Hey, Mommy messed up today. Grown-ups sometimes do, and I'm really sorry."

By allowing our children to see that we're human, that we're attaining from glory to glory as the Bible says (2 Cor. 3:18), and that sometimes we're going to fail despite our best efforts, we give our kiddos permission to be imperfect too. They don't need that pressure any more than we do.

Go ahead and embrace this motherhood thing with all you've got. (Go big or go home, right?) And don't worry about finding those teachable moments. Trust me; they'll find you, and when they do, God will help you speak life into your children—the way He speaks life into you.

God Calls Me Enough (with His Strength)

There are so many times we have mom guilt or feel like we're not doing our best. It's important that we don't try to be perfect in front of our kids, but that we teach them through the hard times. To be a good example to our children, we have to show them how to work through the difficult seasons and how to rejoice during the easy ones. On the days when you feel like you're not enough, remember these words: "But he said to me, 'My grace is sufficient for you, for my power is made perfect in weakness.' Therefore I will boast all the more gladly of my weaknesses, so that the power of Christ may rest upon me" (2 Cor. 12:9 ESV).

It is with God's strength that we parent these precious blessings, and He promises to make you strong in Him.

Teach Your Kids to Love Learning

The library is a fantastic place for your kids to spend time. To encourage learning through books, have your kids choose two nonfiction books for every fiction chapter book they pick out. If your kids are interested in sharks, find online documentaries they can watch. Take them to an aquarium if there is one in your area. Encourage them to explore topics that they find interesting and help them discover new resources.

6

They Call Me Cheerleader

Michelle's Intel

As a full-time freelance journalist, I often had to be very creative finding time to work when my girls were young. This was especially true when I was on deadline. Though I often set my alarm an hour earlier than normal to crank out words or worked like crazy after the girls went to bed, sometimes those additional hours just weren't enough to meet a supertight deadline. That's when my laptop came with us as we traveled from activity to activity.

I'd write while the girls attended art classes, computer camp, and gymnastics team practice. And that was a good plan, most of the time, as long as I understood my role—my cheerleading role. This was never more true than when my girls took the mat for their tumbling passes.

I might be in the middle of crafting a really great paragraph, or studying background information for a series of articles, but when Abby or Ally stood at the end of the long blue row of mats, I knew they'd be checking to see if Mama was watching. Though I was just one drop in the sea of adults seated in the parents' bleachers, my girls only cared if *my* eyes were on them. They wanted to make sure I was watching when they threw their roundoff back handspring series. They wanted me to celebrate with them when they nailed a new trick. They wanted to glance up into the bleachers and see me smiling at them with the thumbs-up sign. And I was more than happy to oblige.

Yes, I needed to work but I also needed to keep my priorities straight. By watching them, cheering for them, and giving them the positive reinforcement they needed, I let Abby and Ally know they were more important than my work. And guess what? They still are. Even though my daughters are in their twenties now, they are still more important than everything else in my life, except for my God and my husband. And they know it.

I'd like to say I've always given my girls the attention due them, but that would be a lie. Even now, I am still attaining in this area. In fact, Abby called me on it not long ago when we met for lunch. After we ordered, I frantically searched my purse for my cell phone, but I couldn't find it.

"Gosh, I can't believe I left my phone charging at home," I said, obviously frustrated, to which Abby answered, "Good. I'm glad you left your phone at home. That means I'll get your undivided attention."

Ouch.

She was right, and you know what? We had a lovely lunch of good conversation, great food, and a lot of laughter. No phones needed.

You see, no matter how old they are, our children still crave our support and approval. They want our time. They want our attention.

The work. The laundry. The housework. Netflix. Facebook and Instagram. They'll always be there. But your children are only this age, at this stage, right now. You can't get today back, so use your minutes wisely.

You've probably heard the quote referring to mommyhood, "The days are long but the years are short." Well, now that I'm Mama of two grown daughters with children of their own, I can testify—that quote is very true. Don't take a minute for granted. Don't miss a chance to celebrate your children. Give them your undivided attention. Be their best cheerleader—day in and day out—and I'm pretty sure when you glance up at your heavenly Father, He will be giving you the thumbs-up sign.

Bethany's JETTliner

Seconds after I plop on the couch with a book or open my laptop to knock some to-dos off my list, a child's voice rings out.

"*Mooooooommmy.*" Depending on the singsong level of the call, someone is either tattling or wants me to watch something.

That *something* is either a YouTube satire of *Frozen* or clips from *America's Funniest Home Videos*. Or, even more dreaded . . . my sons want me to watch them play Minecraft.

"Let me give you a tour of my house!"

Eager faces wait expectantly for me to drop whatever I'm in the middle of doing.

Truthfully, I'm impressed with my children's imaginative creations. Even my youngest child builds incredible houses and castles, complete with multileveled floors, furnished rooms, and roller coasters. Oftentimes, my children have made special houses with pink carpet for me or giant tree-shaped hearts outlining their virtual gardens.

These are the moments that matter.

These are the moments when I can speak words of positivity, encouragement, and admiration into their hearts. The world is going to tear them down so I want to overflow their spirits with words of life.

These are the moments I can build them up.

Their creation is important to them, so it's important to me.

These days I'm watching Fortnite dances and checking out the different skins, but the sentiment is the same.

The precious moments we spend cheering on our kids for their creativity and ability to think outside the box instills confidence in them, letting them know that because we rally for them in the small things, we'll cheer mightily for them in the big ones.

God Calls Me Approved

He says you are a child of the Most High God, and you already have His stamp of approval.

"For the eyes of the Lord are on the righteous and his ears are attentive to their prayer" (1 Peter 3:12). Isn't it wonderful to know that you're already approved by Almighty God? You don't have to earn it, and you can't lose your right standing with Him. He is always watching you, just like a proud parent. I can almost see Him nudging Gabriel and saying, "Look at her go! She's walking in her calling. She's showing unconditional love. She's stepping out in faith!"

Psalm 147:11 says that God takes pleasure in us. In other words, He really likes us. He enjoys us. And He approves of us. Rejoice in those truths today.

Catch Them in the Act . . . and Reward Them!

Here's a fun idea to cheer on your kiddos and reinforce good behavior. If your children are little, get a package of stickers at your local discount store and get ready to play the "I caught you" game.

When you observe your kiddo holding the door open for a sibling, give that child a sticker and say, "I caught you being helpful, so here's your sticker." Give a sticker to your children sitting quietly during a church service and say, "I caught you being a good listener today; here's your sticker." The possibilities are endless. Tell other adults in your world about your "I caught you" game and ask them to help you catch your kids being good. Of course, you'll need to arm those adults with their own sticker stash.

You can offer added rewards: For every ten stickers received, that child gets total control of the remote for an entire day. Or, for every twenty stickers received, that child gets to have a friend over to spend the night. You can give each child a sticker book to keep track of his or her own stickers, or you can chart them on a master sticker board in the kitchen.

This same game works for older children, too, just without the stickers as a reward. Maybe you reward the older children with more screen time or a raise in their allowance. Or you could simply use a "Caught You Being Good" chart to document and praise your children of all ages, with that being reward enough.

Be sure to catch even those kids who are the hardest to catch being good. You will be making a deposit in their memory bank that they will have for a lifetime.

7

They Call Me Fun Sponge

Bethany's JETTliner

I cannot, will not, and repeat, *cannot* forgive my husband for nicknaming me the "Fun Sponge."

Am I the queen of safety?

Yes.

Am I the sponge that soaks all the fun out of the room?

I guess it depends on what your idea of fun is.

For instance, when my youngest was eighteen months old, my former-parachute-rigger husband constructed a zip line in our backyard while I was away on a business trip. Then he strapped said eighteen-month-old into a baby carrier and slid him down.

Filmed it.

Then sent it to me. #DadOfTheYear

I admit that my boys don't think I'm as fun as their daddy because their daddy is a risk taker, fearless and adventurous. All of the qualities that attracted me to him in the first place.

This means I have to work harder at the fun stuff, but guess what? Challenge accepted.

I've made it my mission to teach the boys to delight in the small things.

John 10:10 says that Jesus came to bring life, life to the full. As moms we want our kids to have rich, full lives.

I needed to make a switch so my children could learn to entertain themselves without having to look at a television screen and so they could appreciate the toys they have. It's vital that we teach our kids to find joy in the nonmaterial things like playing games with each other. We found ourselves in a holding pattern of our kids only having fun when we paid for activities or bought them little presents.

Intentional parenting means taking a hard look at our behaviors, and I felt like I was guilty of raising entitled children.

Something had to change.

Now we celebrate the small things instead of the extravagant.

Instead of having a weekly (or, if we're honest, twice-a-week) pizza night, I turned that expectation into a privilege. I want our kids to be excited about the little things instead of taking them for granted.

Once in a while Justin and I will pack up the kids in their pj's and run through a drive-through together to get a late-night sweet treat. Fridays are great nights for this, since the extra sugar burst will keep them up for a little bit.

One strategy that has worked well at our house is Mommy Movie Fun Night, which consists of pizza and junk food, usually chips, dollar boxes of candy from Target, and a two-liter bottle of soda. Then we hunker down in our pj's for the movie of their choice.

Not only has restricting junk food to one special evening helped our budget and waistlines, but the boys get really excited about spending that evening with me . . . although I know the pizza, candy, and soda are the real draw.

It's nice that my kids are learning that fun can be had in the simple things.

Michelle's Intel

I once read an article that said children spell love T-I-M-E. As I pondered that statement, I had to agree. Sometimes, as parents, we think that our kids spell love M-O-N-E-Y because our society has become so materialistic, but in reality, kids have fun just being with us. Growing up, Abby and Ally loved piling on my bed and watching old Doris Day movies. We'd pop buttery popcorn and cuddle under our favorite blankets. My girls loved that more than practically anything else. Even when they got older, they still loved "family time." We'd partner up and play euchre, or we'd head out together for a hike.

The key is to find activities that you and your children enjoy doing together like going fishing, doing crafts, reading stories, baking cookies, playing board games . . . Just find some common ground and make time for your children. Even if you have to "pencil in" a day of fun with your kiddos in your daily planner—do it! Making memories with the people you love most—what could be more fun than that?

God Calls Me Joyful

We should fill our homes with sunshine and laughter. The source of our joy is Jesus. Even when we are stressed or overwhelmed, we can trust that God can fill us internally. Job 8:21 says, "He will yet fill your mouth with laughter, and your lips with shouting" (ESV). Let's allow God to fill our hearts with joy and be an example of that joy to our children so they may be filled as well.

Cheap (or Free!) Activities for Kids

- Bubble "baths" in the kiddie pool
- Nerf gun fights
- Library visits
- Late-night ice cream runs
- Cooking together
- Mommy Movie Fun Nights
- Puzzles
- Dinners out to places where kids eat free
- Local hardware store's free kid workshops
- Reading in a fort
- Pizza picnic under the table
- Origami folding
- Nature scavenger hunts at the park
- Building an obstacle course

8

They Call Me the Worst
Picker-Outer in the World

Michelle's Intel

When my girls were in elementary school, Abby once called me "the worst picker-outer in the world" because I made her take off her white sandals and wear black patent leather shoes with her pink Easter dress. When she whined that black didn't go with pink, I explained it was too cold for sandals and added, "You're not supposed to wear white before Memorial Day anyway" (because that was a fashion rule drilled into my brain by my own mother).

That Easter incident was just the beginning of my reign as worst picker-outer in the world. Allyson, my then six-year-old daughter, so hated the outfits I'd chosen for her to wear while I was away speaking at a conference, she donned a belly shirt and a tutu one morning, trying to convince Daddy that this was the exact outfit I had placed in the baggie marked "Tuesday's outfit for Ally"—which I'd carefully put together for every day I was going to be out of town. When he called her on it, Ally burst into tears and said, "But I can't wear what Mommy laid out for me to wear. It's . . . it's . . . nerdy." (Ironically, Allyson graduated with a degree in fashion from the Fashion Institute of Design & Merchandising—who knew?)

Over the years, I've put up with more than my fair share of eye rolls and sighs of frustration over my fashion choices and advice. (Let's just say neither daughter shares my love of animal print, lol.) And, on more than one occasion, I've been headed out the door only to hear, "Are you going to wear *that*? Oh, Mother . . ." And I've had to be "the bad guy" once in a while and insist they change clothes when their outfit choices were a bit too risqué for my liking. But I've also experienced sacred shopping trips—like picking out that first prom dress, choosing senior picture outfits, and finding the most important dress of all—the wedding gown! You see, even though Abby and Ally might think I'm the worst picker-outer in the world at times, I'm still their mama, and they love me and want my approval.

That's the thing about being a mom; we wear many hats and hold many titles—some good and some not so good—but in the end, we wouldn't trade a single day of this crazy thing we call motherhood.

Sometimes, the decisions we make as moms force us to be the bad guy and hold the titles of unreasonable, ridiculous, mean, not cool, too strict, nerdy, old-fashioned, and worst picker-outer in the world, to name a few. But on those days, the days we feel alone and wounded, remember this: motherhood isn't a popularity contest. We aren't called to be our children's best friend—that role comes later when the children are grown and out on their own. While they're still living in your house, under your rules, the "best friendship" role is on hold. Of course, you want to have fun with your kids at all stages of their lives, but you can't let the desire for them to like you motivate your parenting decisions. Looking back,

I can clearly see that when I focused too much on pleasing my girls, or worrying about them getting upset with me, I would almost always compromise in some way and make a bad parenting decision.

Bottom line, to be a good mom, you have to be the enforcer and the disciplinarian, and, yes, the fun-sucker on occasion. And that's okay. Just know that no matter what less-than-flattering title you've been given by your kiddos today, it will all be worth it in the end. As mamas, we are raising little humans to become amazing adults. Could there be anything more important or challenging in life? I think not. So, give yourself a break and wear that "worst picker-outer in the world" title proudly. Stand your ground, knowing the title "best mom ever" is in your future . . . it just might not be in your immediate future.

Bethany's JETTliner

I'm the worst picker-outer when it comes to presents for my kids. My parents will ask what the boys want for Christmas and immediately I'm thinking of calm, quiet activities like books, drawing pads, and market sets. Or I'll grab a Lego set, but it's not the one that has the right character. And no, I don't know the difference between Marvel and DC comic book characters, although I'm learning.

Meanwhile my husband picks out pogo sticks, skateboards, and at-home science kits.

Michelle is right—we have to pick our battles as moms. Over the years I've become better at choosing my fights, aka, no to the pogo stick, yes to the skateboard *if* there are helmets, knee pads, and wrist guards, and this year I ordered the Scientific Explorer Disgusting Science Kit.

I've had to embrace who God made my kids to be, and my kids love all things ooey-gooey-disgusting and slimy and any activity that could potentially lead to a hospital visit.

But that's who they are, so my prayer is that God helps to shape me as I shape them.

God Calls Me Masterpiece

Ephesians 2:10 says, "For we are God's masterpiece" (NLT). Now that's a title to celebrate! The Creator of the universe thinks we're masterpieces! Dictionary.com defines masterpiece as "a person's greatest piece of work."[3] How about that for a title! So the next time your kiddos label you "worst mom ever" or "totally uncool" or "unreasonable," take a deep breath and remember, God calls you His masterpiece. You are His best work.

A Mom by Any Other Name Is Still Mom

Ever wondered how many names there are for "mom"? I started thinking about this when I was carefully choosing my grandmother name. (I chose Gigi because it sounded less old, lol.) Anyway, I researched the mom name and its many variations, and here's that compiled list for your reading pleasure:

- Mother
- Mom
- Ma
- Mama
- Mum
- Mommy
- Mam
- Mummy
- Motha
- Madre
- Momma
- Mammy
- Maw
- Momushka
- Mummers
- Moo Moo
- MomMom

---

3. Dictionary.com, s.v. "masterpiece," accessed August 2, 2019, https://www.dictionary.com/browse/masterpiece.

9

They Call Me Chef

Bethany's JETTliner

I don't own a salad bowl.

My husband has the boys in Orlando to spend time with family and I'm enjoying some quiet time and watching *NCIS*. Director Vance, a single father, is standing at his pristine countertop tossing veggies in a legit salad bowl.

His onscreen kitchen is beautiful while mine is lived in. Breakfast dishes are in the sink, a pair of chocolate Cheerios guard the coffee maker, and a plastic fork lies on its side in the middle of the tile floor.

Fictional Director Vance is making salad with dinner because that's what television parents do. There is always a salad on the table.

And all I can think about is that I don't have a salad bowl.

It's funny what things we'll focus on or allow to fester in our minds. Not having a salad bowl is no indication of my parenting skills (although the plastic fork that I stepped over instead of picking up might be). And I have bowls that I use for salad, so really, this whole thing is pretty stupid. But it's interesting that it's these little things that settle in our minds.

The underlying issue is that I want to be a good mom and be *seen* as a good mom. Like it or not, much of the ideal parent role model comes from television. We mimic what we like and who we want to be and reject the negative, although the bad can be extremely motivating. The fastest way for me to bleach the entire house is to watch an episode of *Hoarders*.

Maybe you grew up in a house that had a home-cooked meal on the table every night with a beautiful green salad in the middle of the table complete with matching salad tongs. Maybe that's the routine in your house now. I wish it were in mine.

To be completely honest, a lot of our meals aren't eaten formally. There are times Justin and I will get a fancy burger takeout and the kids eat mac and cheese with hot dogs. Or sometimes we're making two sets of meals since the boys won't yet eat zucchini noodles but it's the best pasta substitute for my husband's keto diet. Shouldn't I be happy that my kids are happy and fed and don't go without?

Perhaps that should be enough, but on the days when I spend a couple of hours in the kitchen actually cooking (which I really like to do, FYI), there is a sense of mommy-ness that washes over me. I love when my kids ask me to make homemade meat loaf or frozen buttermilk biscuits with from-scratch sausage gravy. A sense of wholesomeness washes over me as they dig into their plates and I know that I nourished them and fed them and part of me feels complete.

Last year, my husband and I told our boys that we wanted to make sure they knew how to do anything they wanted to learn to do. A month later, our middle child reminded us of that conversation and asked if we would teach him to use the stove.

Do we have a future Michelin star chef in our midst?

We might or might not but if I don't teach him the skills that he wants to learn, I'm hindering what could become a deep love of the culinary arts. It's incredible what kids are able to accomplish when we support them. Just watching an episode of *MasterChef Junior* puts me to shame—I can't cook some of the things those kids can do—and it impresses me that someone took the time to let them learn, create, experiment, and push through the fails so they could focus on the wins.

Having a weekly meal plan is a huge help, and when I spend the time to create one, the week is smoother and there is no dinnertime rush or stress. We save money because we're not in "there's nothing to eat" mode. By allowing our kids to be part of the process, we celebrate meals by appreciating the togetherness . . . whether we have a salad bowl or not.

Michelle's Intel

Let's just say that Jeff didn't marry me for my culinary skills, but I am a pretty good baker. I love to make peanut butter pie, apple crisp pie, double fudge brownies, Southern cream cookies, and my specialty—persimmon pudding. (If you're from the Midwest, you know how yummy that is!)

But my girls will be the first to tell you their mom is not an accomplished chef. I learned to cook a few dishes very well—my Mama's meat loaf, spaghetti casserole, Swiss steak, and buffalo chicken soup. Other than that, I'm the queen of pizza rolls, peanut butter and jelly sandwiches, taquitos, and Bagel Bites. And that's okay.

No #momguilt here. I realized early on in this mama gig that I'm not going to be amazing at everything, and that's just fine by me. Cooking is not my strongest skill, but I can heat up a frozen pizza like a boss, and my kids never went hungry.

If you're in the culinary-challenged mom group, embrace it! Your kids will still love you, and they may just learn to cook so well that you'll never have to host a Thanksgiving dinner at your house.

God Calls Me Provider

Proverbs 31:15 says, "She rises while it is yet night and provides food for her household and portions for her maidens" (ESV). While I love to cook, my baking skills are less than desirable. However, it doesn't matter if some evenings we're eating a homemade and wholesome meal or some nights we're surviving on takeout. I can model the Proverbs 31 woman by making sure my family is full and fed. God calls me to provide nourishment for my children and thankfully there are men and women worldwide who share a plethora of recipes and ideas. Thank you, Pinterest. And when we see another mom who is overwhelmed, let's help her out and send over a casserole (or order a pizza!).

Kid-Friendly Easy Individual Mini Pizzas

Ingredients

- Low-carb tortillas
- Pizza sauce
- Mozzarella (fresh or shredded)
- Grated Parmesan cheese
- Veggies of your choice
- Meats of your choice

Steps

- Preheat your oven to 350 degrees.
- Place the tortillas on a cookie sheet or directly on the oven rack to crisp slightly for a few minutes.
- Remove the tortillas from the oven and place on individual plates.

- Let your kids spread the pizza sauce and add meat and veggie toppings of their choice.
- Sprinkle mozzarella on top of the meat and veggies.
- Sprinkle grated Parmesan on top to create a yummy cheese "crust" and to help it brown.
- Place on cookie sheet and bake until cheese is melted, roughly 5–8 minutes. Optional: put tortilla pizzas under the broiler for 2–3 minutes.
- Remove pizzas from oven and let sit for 2–3 minutes.
- Slice and enjoy!

10

They Call Me Storyteller

Michelle's Intel

As soon as I read in my *What to Expect When You're Expecting* book that my baby had ears and could hear and respond to noises, I grabbed a children's book and started reading to my belly. (Maybe you did the same.) When Abby and Ally were toddlers, I read to them every night, mostly Dr. Seuss books, but we also made up stories of our own. That was always fun because my girls were quite creative and pretty hilarious too! But you know what stories my girls loved the most?

Not the ones written by Dr. Seuss—no offense to the renowned rhyme master because we're all still big Seuss fans. Not the ones we made up together, though they were really funny.

Their favorite stories were the ones about our family—how Jeff and I met when he was a sophomore in high school and I was in eighth grade; how I almost gave birth to Allyson in the hospital parking garage; how Abby tried to be born six weeks early on Halloween; how Mamaw and Papaw met on a blind date; and so on. Sometimes we'd go through old photo albums for hours and I'd narrate, sharing the story behind each picture. Those stories were and still remain my girls' favorite stories—the ones that shaped their lives and the lives of their loved ones.

Some were funny. Some were scary. Some were sad. Some were encouraging. All were entertaining. And some were life changing. Those faith-filled stories are the ones I shared with Abby and Ally most often during their growing-up years, and I continue to do so. In fact, they could probably recite a few of my favorites word for word, but that's good. The Bible says, "So faith comes from hearing, and hearing through the word of Christ" (Rom. 10:17 ESV), so I figure the more they hear these testimony-type stories, the more their faith will increase. Can I get a witness?

When my youngest daughter battled anorexia in high school, I would remind her how the devil had tried to take her out from the very beginning of her life. I'd retell the story of almost miscarrying her and how her very birth took our family to a deeper level of faith. I'd say, "Every time I look at you, Ally, I'm reminded that miracles still happen because you are a living, breathing miracle! The doctor said I'd miscarry you; God said, 'She will live and not die and declare the works of the Lord.' That's why the devil is fighting so hard for your life now. Even he knows that God has a big call on your life, and he isn't too happy about it."

Sharing that story of her miraculous birth would encourage her on those hardest days, and guess what? It still does.

Our minister, Pastor Travis Inman, once pointed out that Hebrews 11 is really just a summary of people's faith stories: Through faith, Abel brought a more acceptable offering than Cain did. By faith Enoch was taken up to heaven without dying. By faith Sarah was able to have a child even though she was barren and old. And then our minister asked, "What's your story?"

At lunch that afternoon, we all talked about our faith stories. Each one of us shared the "God winks" and "divine intervention" moments that had shaped our individual faith walks. It was an amazing afternoon of family, fellowship, and faith.

You see, our children don't care about the theological definitions of faith. They want to know our stories. That's why it's so important that we share our faith stories whenever we have the opportunity. Through our testimonies, we can offer encouragement and hope and build our children's faith.

Keep being a storyteller. Keep reading to your kids. Keep making up stories together. But most importantly, keep sharing your family's stories of faith. Pretty soon, your kiddos will have faith stories of their own to share. Yay!

Bethany's JETTliner

My boys love stories, but like Michelle's daughters, their favorite tales are ones of how Justin and I met, our dating stories, and most important to them, the stories of their births. My husband uploaded tons of photos to our Plex drive. Every once in a while, he'll turn on some music and flip through the pictures. The boys sit fascinated as the images appear on the big screen.

They've learned to recognize one another's baby faces, although the boys look so alike in some of the photos that it takes Justin or me a minute to figure out who is who. We have to look at the background to determine which house we were in or what year the photo was taken to know for sure.

Television shows provide excellent opportunities to share stories. One night we watched a show that presented an opportunity to talk about the dangers of peer pressure and smoking. "You know what, boys," I said. "When I was twelve years old, your Malize"—my mom—"told me she never smoked a puff of a cigarette. Not once. And because she didn't ever do it, I decided I would never do it. And one day a girl asked me at the bus stop if I wanted to smoke."

Their eyes got big at this.

"But do you know what I did?" I asked.

"You didn't do it!" said my oldest.

"That's right. If my mom could never do it, I wanted to be able to say the same thing."

Share your stories . . . the good and the bad *in an age-appropriate manner*. Your story is part of their story and many life lessons are learned from the wisdom we pass on.

God Calls Me a Witness

Revelation 12:11 says, "They triumphed over him by the blood of the Lamb and by the word of their testimony . . ." Testimonies—our faith stories—are powerful. When we share, not only do we build up others' faith, but we also build up our own faith! It's a win-win! C'mon! Be a walking billboard of faith today because your children need to hear your story.

Teach Kids to Share Their Stories

Typically, young children are Chatty Cathys, ready to share every detail of their lives with anyone who will listen, but something happens at about age nine. During those tween years, most everything embarrasses even very outgoing children. Because of the awkwardness of that age, it's often difficult for our kids to share their own stories, their own testimonies, their own faith journeys.

Here's how you can help. Be that "faith prodder" by asking these questions:

- What was your life like before you became a Christian?
- How do you feel differently now compared to before you started living for God?
- Can you think of any specific examples of how your life is different or better than it was before you were a Christian?

After your children answer those questions, say, "That's it! That's your story! That's your testimony, and it's amazing!" Encourage your kiddos to share that exact information with others when questioned about their faith.

11

They Call Me Just Like Mom

Bethany's JETTliner

Carpet is a magnet for vomit.

After two weeks of passing the tummy-flu virus to one another, my precious babies gave it to me. I missed a writers conference where I was scheduled to teach while my dad and stepmom Kathy let me lie in a dark room in peace, fed me applesauce, and took care of my boys since my amazing husband was serving our country overseas.

After almost a week, I was on the mend. My dad went home so he could guest preach at his church and Kathy stayed behind to help me with the boys. The tummy flu also stayed behind and that night my youngest son did not make it to the bathroom before blowing chunks across the beige carpet of the house we rent.

Let me tell you something. When the military moves are over and we finally buy a house, there will be zero carpeting. Although by that time the boys may be out of the house and cleaning up puke will no longer be a job for me, but hey.

After hearing the violent explosion, Kathy and I raced upstairs. "Go take care of him," she said. "I've got this." And she grabbed the paper towels that were fortuitously still in the boys' room, got on her hands and knees, and started cleaning up the vomit.

And I froze.

I was stuck in this weird *Matrix*-like moment. My little one was now retching into the toilet and crying, "I'm sorry, Mommy," as Kathy was bent over the bodily fluids of a grandchild that wasn't blood-related to her.

She looked at me as I stood frozen between the two situations and said, "Go. He needs you."

I let go of the hostessing-guilt and took care of my baby.

Kathy was selfless. She could have easily helped my boy wipe his face and rinse his mouth and given him hugs. Out of the two options, comforting him was definitely the more attractive one. Yet she chose the gross and smelly and disgusting job . . . and actually, she didn't have to do any of it. She was a guest in my home, and cleaning up puke was my job. In fact, at one time I used to reach out my cupped hands when my babies gagged, some strange parenting instinct to catch their spit-up that I'll never understand.

I got my son into bed and then knelt by Kathy's side as we Shop-Vac'd as much moisture out of the carpet as possible. At that moment, I felt so loved.

I know not all stepmother stories are wonderful and certainly fairy tales haven't helped matters. Blending families can be stressful and over-emotional. There's baggage to deal with and no two situations are the same. I know that being a stepparent to adult children is drastically different than becoming a stepmom to children you help raise.

Kathy chose to love me like she loves her own kids, and not only did I respect her for it, I loved her for it.

The bottom line when it comes to loving people is that we have to show it. We have to be there for each other when it hurts . . . and when you literally feel like you're going to vomit because you're cleaning up vomit.

The Bible says not to love each other with word or speech but in deeds and in truth (see 1 John 3:18). Our actions are what melt hearts and break down walls. Our actions are proof of our love and when we feel like we have nothing left to give, we still give anyway. Because we're moms, regardless if the word *step* precedes that title or not.

Michelle's Intel

If you stroll through the mom card section at a Hallmark store, you'll see not only cards for moms but also cards for stepmoms and a section of "just like a mom" cards. I'm so thankful for the women in my life who are "just like a mom" to my daughters. Because let's face it—we mamas could all use a little extra help on this parenting journey! Can I get an amen? Brenda Nolan, otherwise known as Mama Nolan at our house, definitely fits into the "just like a mom" category for us.

Abby and Ally both had Mama Nolan as their high school science teacher, but they learned way more than scientific facts from this wonderful woman. I have no doubt she kept them on the straight and narrow when they were less than enthusiastic about taking advice from me.

Even though both girls have now graduated from high school and college, their bond with Mama Nolan remains. In fact, when we needed help decorating the large outdoor wedding venue for Abby's wedding, Mrs. Nolan (who is amazing at that kind of thing) worked hours and hours, helping us pull it all together in time for the big day. She also threw Abby a beautiful baby shower last year. We love her, and we are so thankful for her spunk, wisdom, humor, and guidance over the years. She is someone the girls know they can always count on, besides me, and that makes this mama feel very blessed. We need more Mama Nolans in the world—folks who are willing to do whatever it takes. I challenge you to bless those "other mothers" in your children's lives and maybe see if you can fill that need for someone else's children.

God Calls Me to Act

Joseph was Jesus's stepfather but we rarely think of him that way. Jesus was Mary's son but had no bloodline from Joseph. Yet Joseph protected Jesus as if he were his own, whisking Mary and the baby to Egypt to escape Herod's decree to kill little boys. James 2:18 says that faith without works is dead: "Show me your faith apart from your works, and I will show you my faith by my works" (ESV). We may find ourselves in situations that are awkward and uncomfortable with our families, but we can always trust that our actions will speak volumes and prove our love for each other.

Christian Books and Resources for Stepmoms

- *But I'm Not a Wicked Stepmother! Secrets of Successful Blended Families* by Kathi Lipp and Carol Boley
- *The Smart Stepmom: Practical Steps to Help You Thrive* by Ron L. Deal and Laura Petherbridge
- *Blended Families: Creating Harmony as You Build a New Home Life* by Maxine Marsolini
- TheSmartStepmom.com with Laura Petherbridge
- HelpClubformoms.com/ministry-of-a-christian-stepmom

12

They Call Me Embarrassing

Michelle's Intel

Okay, I admit it. I desperately wanted to be "the cool mom." You know, the mom all the other kids *wish* was their mom. And I worked hard at it. I always tried to be "the hostess with the mostest" when Abby and Ally had their friends over, and I tried not to wear anything that screamed, "I'm an '80s lady and I don't care who knows it." All in all, I was pretty successful. But once in a while, even "the cool mom" does something completely embarrassing. (You're thinking of your most embarrassing mommy moment right now, aren't you?)

On this particular rainy afternoon, the girls and I were having a mother-daughter day at the local movie theater. We'd already looked up the movie choices on the way to the theater and had decided we'd see *Balls of Fury*, a comedy about the ultimate Ping-Pong tournament starring Christopher Walken. Ally, who had just started her eighth grade year, and Abby, who had just begun her freshman year of high school, both wanted to see *Superbad*. But it was rated R, so I had vetoed that selection even though they'd tried their best to convince me *Superbad* wasn't really that . . . bad.

While waiting in the long ticket line, the girls noticed several of their friends were also there to enjoy a movie and escape the rain. In fact, it seemed the entire theater lobby was filled with their classmates, including the young man about to sell us our tickets. He was in Abby's class. I could tell both girls thought he was cute by the way they were acting.

Finally, it was our turn. I don't know if it was all the prior discussion about *Superbad* or simply an unfortunate mistake, but when the young man asked me what movie we wanted to see, I loudly proclaimed, "Three for *Superballs*."

Both girls gasped.

The young man, who was laughing so hard he could barely speak, said, "Uh, ma'am. We don't have a movie playing by that name . . . Did you mean *Superbad* or perhaps *Balls of Fury*?"

"Yes, *Balls of Fury*," Abby answered, "that's what she meant."

There was no recovering from *Superballs*, so I simply paid and we bolted to theater number three, which wasn't playing *Balls of Fury* or *Superbad*. It was playing *Underdog*, which seemed fitting since I was going to be in the doghouse with my girls for a long time. On the plus side, none of their classmates were in *Underdog* so they didn't have to see any of them and relive what will forever be known as "the *Superballs* moment."

Let's face it. You're going to embarrass your children at some point in their lives, and possibly at some point every day once middle school is in full swing. But that's okay. You'll survive those embarrassing mom moments, and though your children might not think they will live through them, they will also be just fine. And here's more good news. Those embarrassing *Superballs* moments will eventually become the family memories you recall often, share with others, and laugh about until your bellies hurt.

The Bible tells us in Ecclesiastes that there is a time to laugh, and it says in Proverbs 17:22 that a cheerful heart is good medicine. Bottom line, the sooner you learn to laugh at yourself, the better. Don't be so serious all the time. Lighten up, sister!

You can't be perfect every day, and even if you could be, you'd still embarrass your children somehow because that's just how it works. I think it's their rite of passage to be embarrassed by us. It doesn't mean your kiddos love you any less; it just means they're growing up. When they're little, they look at you adoringly and love you unconditionally. Once they hit middle school? Not so much. They will secretly still adore you, but you'll have to know that truth in your knower and remind yourself of it on those *Superballs* kind of days.

Looking back on the many embarrassing mom moments in my life, I can't help but smile. At the time, messing up seemed monumental, but now they're just funny memories woven into this beautiful tapestry we call motherhood. So don't be too hard on yourself the next time you embarrass your children. Meditate on that sweet home décor sign you probably have hanging in your family room right now, "Live. Laugh. Love," and do all three. Remember that our shortcomings and parental failures may embarrass our kids, but they don't embarrass God; they simply qualify us for a healthy dose of His love and grace.

Bethany's JETTliner

Now that my kids are hyperaware of their peers, I've found that the threat of embarrassment is an interesting behavior-changing tactic. They've embarrassed me for years in public so I feel no regret when I turn the tables on them. At the first sign of misbehavior or sibling fighting, I beckon them to me, lean down, and whisper, "Do you want to stand in the corner in front of all your friends?"

Their eyes bug out of their faces. "No, ma'am."

"Then *stop it*."

Bim. Bam. Boom. Ninety-nine percent of the time, the boys adjust their behavior because they know I'll follow through.

The trick was following through when they were younger.

As children of a youth minister, the boys grew up in church and spent many hours there. During the week they ran and played in the gym freely, but on Wednesday nights, the tables were set up for meals and the room was crowded. Running, jumping, and yelling were not appropriate, yet sometimes they forgot.

And sometimes they disobeyed after being warned.

And sometimes they had to put their noses on the wall during the meal.

I'm not advocating intentional humiliation, but embarrassment can be a powerful motivator for behavior. Don't be afraid to use it.

God Calls Me His Workmanship

Your kids may be embarrassed by you at times, but God calls you His workmanship—even on your most embarrassing mom-fail kind of days. In other words, He isn't embarrassed by you one bit. Ephesians 2:10 says, "For we are his workmanship, created in Christ Jesus for good works, which God prepared beforehand, that we should walk in them" (ESV). Be encouraged. God has enough love and grace to cover even your biggest embarrassments.

It's Good to Laugh . . . Even If You're the Source of Amusement

The average four-year-old laughs three hundred times a day while the average forty-year-old only laughs seventeen times a day. Those statistics have been reported in publications around the globe, from the *Times* to the *Huffington Post*, though some say those stats are nothing more than an urban myth. Still, regardless of the authenticity of those statistics, here's the truth: as adults we need to laugh more.

And as moms we definitely need to laugh more.

Not only does the Bible say a merry heart is good like medicine, but also science backs that up! Read on!

- Laughter is good for your heart: According to a study at the University of Maryland Medical Center, laughter may help prevent heart disease. The study found that people with heart disease were 40 percent less likely to laugh in a variety of situations compared to people of the same age without heart disease.[4]

- Laughter is a good workout: It has been proven that hearty laughter burns calories, equivalent to several minutes on a rowing machine or an exercise bike. And, let's face it, laughing is way more fun than rowing.

- Laughter can enhance learning: Laughter stimulates both sides of the brain to enhance learning. In fact, laughter eases muscle tension and psychological stress, which keeps the brain alert and allows people to retain more information.

You know, researchers suggest that we need a minimum of twelve laughs per day just to stay healthy. So, go ahead. Laugh it up, because a lack of humor in your life is no laughing matter.

---

4. "Laughter Is Good for Your Heart, According to a New University of Maryland Medical Center Study," ScienceDaily, November 17, 2000, https://www.sciencedaily.com/releases/2000/11/001116080726.htm.

13

They Call Me Exhausted

Bethany's JETTliner

Caffeine was invented for moms burning the candle at both ends.

When I started the Serious Writer Academy, we were living in a small apartment that cost more than half of our monthly income. Freelance money became our saving grace as we waited for Justin's military school seat to open up. In the meantime, he worked two jobs and took night courses to earn networking certifications while I finished my undergrad and taught myself how to build websites, email lists, and grow a company from scratch.

Caffeine became my drug of choice.

Coffee in the morning. Coffee in the evening. Naps in between.

This crazy cycle is the epitome of survival mode.

Fortunately, my boys saw firsthand what true hustle and grit look like.

Unfortunately, well-intentioned family and friends who lived and died by the nine-to-five workplace model criticized and teased about my "sleeping in," even though I hadn't gone to bed until 5:00 a.m.

My inner circle grew smaller as my awake hours grew longer and I declined invitations to go out.

It felt like the schedule I had when my sons were infants. In between feeding the boys and chores, I'd sneak a nap and insist the boys rest as well.

When Justin deployed, I found solace in the quiet hours after the boys went to sleep. As an introvert, I craved the times where I was responsible to no one and alone with my thoughts.

The more I worked during the night, the more time I could spend with the kids during the day. However, this system can last for only so long before your health starts to suffer.

Sleep is crucial for brain function, healthy weight maintenance, and improved moods.

I became guilty of coveting the quiet hours so much that I sacrificed sleep, which turned me into a walking Mombie, irritable and tired all the time.

If you're in a crazy cycle, give yourself permission to go to bed. Our brains require sleep to flush out all the information and data processed throughout the day. Neuroscientist Jeff Iliff gave a fantastic TED talk about how the glymphatic system in our brains is a natural cleansing process.[5] The one requirement: sleep.

Jesus demonstrated the importance of rest during His life on earth. When He was on the boat with His disciples, a great storm tossed the boat to the point where the well-sea-traveled fishermen were frightened. Jesus slept through the whole thing until the disciples woke Him. I always wondered if Jesus went back to sleep after He calmed the waves and rebuked the disciples.

---

5. Jeff Iliff, "How Does Our Brain Get Rid of Toxins?" National Public Radio, *TED Radio Hour*, October 21, 2016, https://www.npr.org/2016/10/21/497849178/how-does-our -brain-get-rid-of-toxins.

The military places importance on sleep as well. There are times when Justin is required to have *x* hours of sleep before performing certain tasks. Lucky for him, his Marine Corps training is so instilled that he can sleep anywhere and fall asleep in an instant.

Sometimes we are in seasons of busyness. If that's your situation, give yourself grace. Take naps. Rest. Refresh your soul.

I used to look at sleep as a waste of time. The hours spent sleeping were hours I could be working. However, I put my family at a disadvantage. That thinking had to change.

When you fly on an airplane, the flight attendant's instructions are always the same. If the oxygen masks fall from the ceiling, put the mask on your face first, then help others. You are no good to anyone if you are unconscious.

The same idea applies to us as moms.

We give so much of ourselves to our families and jobs that we deplete our resources. If we don't take the time to recuperate, we can't help anyone else. Our health must be at the forefront, which is easier said than done, I admit.

God also calls us to rest and gave us this example when He created the world (see Genesis 2). He didn't rest because He was tired, for Isaiah 40:28 says that God never faints nor grows weary. Instead, the word *rest* can mean *to cease*, or *stop*.

We have to stop.

My kids would definitely agree that I'm in a season when I'm Tired Mommy, but with intentional self-care, I can change this mind-set.

I want to be the energetic mommy.

Won't you join me in scheduling some "me time" on the calendar to read, nap, write, take a walk, or enjoy a hobby that recharges your spirit?

Caffeine optional.

Michelle's Intel

So you know you need to get more shut-eye, but you just can't seem to sleep when it's time for bed, right? It's a common problem, especially for moms, because even though our bodies are crying out for sleep, we can't turn off our minds. If you're like me, I'm going over tomorrow's to-do list in my head, which can often lead to worrying over whether I'll actually accomplish all the items on that list. One strategy that has helped me is having a notebook on my nightstand. Right before going to sleep, I write down my to-do list for the next day so I won't have to keep going over it in my head.

Here are ten more sleep strategies that should help you drift off to dreamland:

1. Exercise regularly—but not within three hours of going to bed.
2. Spray some lavender linen spray on your sheets—but not too much.
3. Try some bedtime relaxation techniques, deep breathing, sinking into the bed, and so on.
4. Take a warm bath before bedtime.
5. Maintain a relaxing atmosphere in the bedroom.
6. Establish a bedtime ritual.
7. Leave your phone charging in a different room so you won't be tempted to play on it.
8. Start decreasing liquids several hours before bedtime so you won't have to pee during the night.
9. Use a white noise machine or simply run a fan or play soothing music at bedtime.
10. Meditate on Proverbs 3:24: "When you lie down, you will not be afraid; when you lie down, your sleep will be sweet."

God Calls Me to Rest

Isaiah 40:31 says, "Those who hope in the LORD will renew their strength. They will soar on wings like eagles; they will run and not grow weary, they will walk and not be faint." Our bodies and our souls require periods of rest. The next time we feel pressured to pull an all-nighter or feel exhausted, let's remember that our heavenly Father is the one who refreshes our spirits and promises to give us strength through Him.

Power Nap Tip

Create a "rest box" of toys or activities that your kids can only play with during rest time. Set an alarm for twenty-five minutes, hand your kids the box, and enjoy some uninterrupted relaxation.

14

They Call Me Chauffeur

Michelle's Intel

When my daughters were little, I enrolled them in gymnastics lessons. I knew it would be good for their coordination no matter what sport they ended up pursuing in school, and if they wanted to follow in my cheerleading footsteps, I knew they'd need to master back handsprings and back tucks. Plus, I was hoping an hour at gymnastics would tire them out and make our bedtime routine a little easier. So, they started lessons in Fort Worth, Texas, where we lived, but when their favorite gymnastics instructors moved to an All-Star Cheerleading gym in Decatur, we decided to follow them. Sure, it was about a forty-five-minute drive, but my parents lived in Decatur so we saw this as a win-win—learning from great gymnastics and cheer coaches at a prestigious gym and spending time with Mamaw and Papaw.

Yes, that forty-five-minute drive each way was a challenge three times a week, but I was determined to make those minutes count. After questioning the girls about their day at school and going over any homework we could talk through, I would put on music and we would sing at the top of our lungs. Some days it was the greatest hits of the '80s. (To this day, Abby and Ally know every word to John Mellencamp's "Small Town.") Some days it was *Doris Day's Greatest Hits* and we'd belt out the lyrics to "Teacher's Pet." Other days, we sang along with Sinatra. But every single time we made that trek to Decatur, the girls insisted on one particular CD, and it wasn't "I Won't Eat That" by Willy Welch, though they liked that one. It was Christian singer Janny Grein's *Anthology Collection*, and they'd ask me to put "Covenant Woman" on repeat. Some days, that was the only song we listened to the entire way there and back.

I'd get so tickled looking in my rearview mirror at five-year-old Allyson, singing into her thumb as if it were a microphone, eyes closed, crooning, "I'm not moved by what I feel. Oh, I'm only moved by the Word that's real . . ." Then Abby would chime in with her Texas twang, "I'm a Covenant wuuuuhman . . ."

And you know what? All those hours back and forth to Decatur, singing faith-infused songs, did a whole lot more for them than I could have ever imagined. You see, I thought I was just taking them to a new gym to master new tumbling skills, but God was using that drive time to build in them a new identity. For many hours, they sang about being a covenant woman, and today they both are!

Abby married a worship minister and they serve at a large church in Lexington, Kentucky. I love to watch Abby worship as her husband ushers the congregation into the very presence of the Lord. Allyson married her high school sweetheart, and she serves God in the marketplace as a product development specialist with Adidas. She's traded in her faith-filled music for powerful podcasts from her favorite preachers on her commute to and from work, but she is truly a covenant woman in every way.

I'll be honest. Several of my family members thought it was ridiculous for us to drive forty-five minutes one way three days a week for cheer and gymnastics lessons, and they were quite vocal about telling me so. One even criticized that I had my priorities messed up, putting too much emphasis on a sport that would hold no eternal value. *But God* can see the beginning and the end and all of the in-betweens, and He had a plan.

Say that out loud right now, wherever you are: "But God."

Maybe I did have my priorities out of whack.

But God.

Maybe I could've found a gym closer to home.

But God.

You see, I wouldn't trade those minutes with my daughters in our sanctified SUV for anything in the world. We grew closer to God and to one another during those treks to Decatur, and we spent quality time with Mamaw and Papaw, who went to heaven not too many years after that season. Looking back, those dinners at my parents' home in Decatur three times a week were just an added blessing.

If you're the chauffeur these days, carting your kids to and from a gazillion activities, why not use those minutes to connect with the Master? Sing praise songs. Memorize Scripture together. Listen to Word-packed podcasts. Pray together (eyes open, of course). Or simply connect with your kiddos, really listening to them and imparting words of wisdom and words of affirmation into their little hearts.

After all, our greatest job is to raise our children to be covenant men and covenant women with their feet planted deep in the Word of God. Let's not waste any minutes or any miles.

Bethany's JETTliner

The best part of driving your children is that they are forced to interact with you. They're literally strapped inside a Mommy-Wants-to-Talk Mobile. It's genius. It's also a great time to listen.

My boys love to sing so we'll connect our iPhones to the Bluetooth speaker and belt out our favorite songs from Amazon Music. Lately we've been listening to *The Greatest Showman* soundtrack on repeat and we've loved every minute of it.

Occasionally my boys ask me to play specific songs from the soundtrack. As they belted out the words they knew and mumbled over the rest, I took the opportunity to really listen to the meaning behind the songs.

What about this song meant something to them?

And when the song ended, I asked.

And listened.

Now the trick to being able to listen to little boys talk about subjects that they didn't initiate means that questions can never be answered with a simple *yes* or *no*.

And as we started talking about dreams and goals, I encouraged them to share their hearts by asking follow-up questions and respecting their answers enough by not discouraging their ideas.

The car is a valuable resource—take advantage of it. After all, sooner than we'd like, our kids won't need us to be their chauffeur and we'll lose those precious teaching moment opportunities.

God Calls Me to Trust Him

You may not have it all figured out, and your family and friends may not always agree with your parenting decisions, but that's okay. Because if you're following God and trusting Him with your children, you don't have to have all the answers. Isaiah 55:8–9 says, "'For my thoughts are not your thoughts, neither are your ways my ways,' declares the LORD. 'As the heavens are higher than the earth, so are my ways higher than your ways and my thoughts than your thoughts.'" I love these verses because they show me even though I think I'm just driving my kids to and from the gym, He has a higher plan. We can rest in that truth and begin thanking Him for all the "But God" moments in our lives.

Pack Snacks

A successful commute or road trip with kids has to have one essential thing: snacks. And not just any snacks—healthy snacks that aren't too messy for the car. Of course, you'll want to avoid any of the below items if they are foods your child is allergic to, but if there are no food allergies, these snacks will be easy to grab and go:

- Raisins
- A protein shake or bar
- Almonds
- Peanut butter and jelly sandwiches
- Granola bars
- Apple slices
- Popcorn
- Trail mix
- Jell-O
- Crackers and hummus
- Carrots
- Celery sticks

Lastly, you'll want to keep an emergency backpack in the car with extra changes of clothes for each child, bandages and alcohol wipes, water bottles, a flashlight, batteries and chargers for cell phones, toilet paper, baby wipes, a battery-powered or hand-crank radio, a blanket, and extra snacks like crackers and granola bars. It's always best to be prepared.

15

They Call Me Beautiful

Bethany's JETTliner

"Mommy, you're a princess."

All of life's stresses vanished at that moment. My little boy looked at me from his cozy spot on the couch. He hugged his bear's neck and smiled. I shut the front door, placed the mail on top of the entertainment unit, and scooched close to him. The smell of baby lotion and shampoo was still fresh on his skin from his post-playtime bath.

"Thank you, baby," I said. "I love you so much." I kissed his little face, smoothed his hair off his forehead, and patted his back.

He shifted slightly. "And Daddy is Shrek."

Shrek?

Only then did I turn my attention to the movie he was watching . . . the movie that was supposed to induce sleepiness for naptime.

And only then did I realize that my precious angel who thought I was a princess was watching *Shrek 2*, where beautiful Fiona is no longer a human, but an ogre. A large green-warted ogre.

Aren't kids innocent?

My son saw past Fiona's exterior to who she was, and to him, she was still the heroine of the movie, the beautiful princess. And that's the compliment he was passing to me.

Why can't I see myself the way my kids see me?

I've looked into my little boys' eyes enough times to see the purest, most unselfish love I have ever known. There are no strings, no hidden motives. They just love their mama. And in that moment, my baby was telling me that too.

But oh so often, I see myself as ogre Fiona and I act accordingly.

I don't always want to leave the house because I'm not appropriately dressed or my hair is on day three of needing to be washed and the dry shampoo isn't fooling anyone.

I don't want to wear a swimsuit because the years of bad food choices are obvious in latex and I'm not ready to wear the skirted suit option.

I take pictures of my kids instead of me *with* my kids.

More than seeing myself the way my kids see me, I should look at myself the way God sees me. He created us in His image and while we can speculate about what that means on an external level, we know that it means our souls are created to be like Him.

In my opinion, God is a fan of beauty. Instead of leaving the earth brown and blue, He decorated with color, texture, and pattern. The universe is sprinkled with glittering stars and planets. Animals come in every shape and size. Why do we think that we, His crown of creation, are any less than these?

That's why it's important for us to care about our image. We are a reflection of the God who made us and the Christ who died for us. What message do we send our children and the world if we don't respect ourselves enough to take care of ourselves?

Don't get me wrong. There's a balance here and sometimes I am too hard on myself when it comes to feeling beautiful. When those moments come, I need to remind myself that no matter how pretty I may appear on the outside, it's the beauty of my character that matters. My children prefer a mommy who is kind, compassionate, fun, and strong. It wouldn't matter to them if I were Miss America if my personality was unlovable.

So I'll get in the photos with my children and I'll think less of myself when they ask me to play outside or be by the pool. Any lumps or bumps that I'm hyperaware of don't matter to my kids. One day those requests will fade, and I don't want to regret wasting the moments they asked to spend time with me.

Michelle's Intel

Seriously, is there anything more humbling than standing in front of a dressing room mirror, under those unforgiving fluorescent lights, trying on a bathing suit? I think not. I dread it every year. Because no matter how many miles you've logged on the treadmill in previous months . . . no matter how many crunches you've crunched . . . no matter how many desserts you've passed up . . . bathing suits show every imperfection. While you might be able to hide a few dimples underneath Spanx leggings or a nice black dress, you're not hiding anything in a bathing suit.

That's pretty much how it is with God. You might be able to fake-grin your way through church, and "play Christian" in front of your friends and family, but when you enter the throne room, it's like wearing your bathing suit before God. You can't hide any imperfections! He sees it all. That truth used to horrify me—even more than trying on bathing suits—but not anymore. Because once we ask Jesus to forgive our sins and be the Lord of our lives, God sees us through "the Jesus filter," and all He sees is perfection.

It's kind of like how our precious children see us. They don't see all the blemishes and bulges we see—they just see the mommy they love—and to them, we are beautiful.

Now, if we can just figure out some kind of perfection filter for bathing suit season . . .

God Calls Me Beautiful

First Samuel 16:7 says, "People look at the outward appearance, but the LORD looks at the heart." God made us in His own image so we should never make fun of others or belittle ourselves. Let's strive to be beautiful on the inside and take care of our bodies as holy and pleasing unto the Lord.

How to Do the "Five-Minute Face" to Feel Your Best

On some mornings there is not enough time to shower, let alone put on makeup. And if we're being honest, our kids don't give a teddy bear's behind if we have mascara on our eyelashes or not. However, when you look better, you feel better, and you're more likely to run a quick errand or open the door for the UPS guy if you're not worried about how you look. At least, that's definitely the case for me.

The five-minute face is a quick morning routine:

1. Wash your face (or use facial cleansing cloths) to remove the sleeping sweat.
2. Apply sunscreen and moisturizer (some products combine SPF + moisturizer + tint).
3. Use foundation or powder as part of your skin-care routine. Let the dirt and pollution stick to your foundation, not your skin.

4. Apply a coat of mascara.

5. Brush your teeth.

6. Apply second coat of mascara.

7. Apply lip gloss.

8. Throw hair in messy bun or put on a baseball cap.

Done!

16

They Call Me Pray-er

Michelle's Intel

Dorsie was not only our neighbor across the street but also my sister's mother-in-law. So while we weren't really related, we felt like we were. She watched over our house when we were away, and we were happy to help her with any household tasks she struggled with because of her age, although she was still pretty feisty for someone in her eighties.

Dorsie was always doing sweet things for my girls, like making them special treats for every holiday, and let me tell you, Dorsie could cook! She loved Abby and Ally, and they loved her.

Because we were sort of related, we were often at family celebrations together. On this particular day, we had all gathered at the local steakhouse for a family birthday luncheon. The girls, who were just three and five at the time, were sharing an order of French fries and bickering over who had more, when all of a sudden, Dorsie collapsed. The next few moments were a blur. Dorsie was lying flat on her back on the floor. My sister was calling 911. The waitress was combing the restaurant to see if anyone with a medical background could help. And the rest of us were standing around, talking about what could've caused her to collapse.

Everyone except Ally.

I panicked when I realized I couldn't find my youngest daughter. She had been right next to me, holding her sister's hand, a minute before. Then I saw her. She was kneeling right next to Dorsie, holding *her* hand.

Ally stayed with Dorsie until the EMTs came. After Ally rejoined our group, her daddy asked, "What were you doing, Al?"

"Praying to Jesus," she answered.

It was as simple as that.

All of our first instincts were to talk about what was happening, to try to figure out why it might have happened, and to call for medical help. Ally's first instinct was to call for help of a Divine nature. She was on assignment, and her prayers were answered—Dorsie recovered.

We all learned a lesson that day from a faith-filled three-year-old: make prayer your first instinct.

Let your children see your prayer life in action.

For example, if you are chauffeuring your kids to an activity and the sunset is especially beautiful, say right out loud, "Thank You, Lord, for such a lovely sunset tonight. You're amazing." Or, if you receive word that someone you know needs immediate prayer support, involve your children in that prayer time. Let them know their prayers are effective and important. Don't just reserve prayer for your bedtime ritual; make prayer an integral part of your everyday life. As you know, our children are always watching us and often imitating our behavior. Wouldn't it be great if they became prayer warriors because they were following our example?

When best-selling author and expert on prayer Stormie Omartian talks to children about prayer, she shares a true story about her washing machine.

"One day my washing machine just quit working," Omartian told me when I interviewed her a few years ago for an article that ran in the Bedford *Times-Mail* newspaper. "I called the repairman to come and take a look at it, and when he did, he discovered that it just needed one tiny little part to fix that big machine.

"I tell kids that the body of believers is like my washing machine, and they are like that tiny, little part. Things don't run well without their prayers."

Omartian, author of *The Power of a Praying Parent*, *The Power of a Praying Teen*, and *The Power of a Praying Kid*, to name only a few of her popular books, wants children to understand that even though they're little, their prayers have a big impact.

"I let them know that their prayers are powerful and very important to God," she adds, noting that the Bible says the kingdom of God belongs to them. "Kids need to know that their prayers matter."

My grown daughters and my grandkids need to know their prayers matter. And your kids need to know their prayers matter. Let's tell them today.

Bethany's JETTliner

It's important that we teach our kids to pray before they eat and before they go to bed, but perhaps more important is teaching them to pray without ceasing and to recognize opportunities throughout the day to praise God for the blessings and to pray for others.

When my husband was deployed we prayed for his safety constantly. However, if the unthinkable happened, I didn't want our boys to blame God. So during our prayers, I made sure to add, "Please keep Daddy safe, dear God. Put legions of angels around him and protect him like You promise in Psalm 91. But even if something happens to him, we know that You love us and care for us and You will be with us."

That's a hard prayer to pray, but it's important for our children to know that God is not a genie wish-granter and sometimes terrible tragedies happen. To encourage them to pray constantly, there are a couple of situations where I demonstrate "intentional prayer" with my kids.

The first is when we're driving and hear an ambulance or fire truck siren. "Boys, we need to pray," I'll say, and then I pray out loud for the people in trouble, that God would separate the traffic so help can arrive as fast as possible, and that no one is seriously injured. I want the siren to become a trigger for the boys to think about others and to intercede on their behalf.

Last week I came home from a conference and my son grabbed my hand. "We heard an ambulance yesterday, Mommy. We prayed for them." I gave him a big hug and then scooped his brothers into my arms as well.

"I'm so proud of you boys," I said, and kissed the tops of their heads . . . no small feat now that my oldest is eye level with me.

The second intentional prayer time is before a call, meeting, or big event. "Daddy has a big meeting today. Let's pray for him." Many times, I'll walk out of my office and draw the boys to me. "I've got an important call with a client. Can you guys pray for me so I'm not nervous?" The boys bow their heads and pray favor over the appointment.

I covet their prayers. The innocence of their requests and their expectance that God hears them means everything.

God Calls Me Nonstop Pray-er

First Thessalonians 5:16–18 says, "Always be joyful. Never stop praying. Be thankful in all circumstances, for this is God's will for you who belong to Christ Jesus" (NLT). In other words, God wants us to stay in constant communication with Him. Pray without ceasing and encourage your kids to do the same.

Five Tips to Writing Your Own Prayers

Here are five tips to help you pen powerful prayers for your family.

1. *Always begin your prayer with praise to God.* For example, say, "Father, we praise You for sending Your Son, Jesus, to die on the cross for our sins. We love You so much."

2. *Be specific with your requests.* For example, don't just pray for peace in the family. Instead, pray: "God, I ask that You cause my children to love one another the way that You love them. Let them always see the best in one another and enjoy spending time together."

3. *Use Scripture in your prayers.* Instead of praying, "Lord, I ask that You cause people to stop talking about me," pray, "Lord, I thank You that no weapon formed against me shall prosper and every tongue that rises against me shall be stilled." (Remember, Jeremiah 1:12 tells us that God watches over His Word to perform it.)

4. *Believe when you pray.* Don't just say the words without believing that God can really answer your requests. Pray expecting! After you've made your request known to God, thank Him for the desired result. Hebrews 11:6 says, "It is impossible to please God without faith. Anyone who wants to come to him must believe that God exists and that he rewards those who sincerely seek him" (NLT). Also, check out Matthew 21:22 and Mark 11:24.

5. *Pray in Jesus's name.* Some have prayed, "For Jesus's sake" and "All God's people said amen" to close their prayers, but the Bible clearly tells us to pray in Jesus's name. In John 16:23 Jesus says, "And in that day you will ask Me nothing. Most assuredly, I say to you, whatever you ask the Father in My name He will give you" (NKJV).

17

They Call Me Road Trip Taker

Bethany's JETTliner

In the last few years, I've driven my kids across the country numerous times and have taken road-tripping to the next level. Thus, I've honed my skills as an extreme road trip taker, emphasis on the word *extreme*.

My ultimate goal is to stop as little as possible, so in the wee hours of the morning, I strap my babies in the car with their pj's still on, shoes on the floor, and blankets and pillows snuggled around them so that we get a jump start on the early rush-hour traffic. If we're stopping at a hotel, I like to arrive around four or five o'clock so we can grab some fast food and spend a relaxing evening in our hotel room.

As a bonus, if we leave early enough, the boys will sleep for a few hours, which means fewer "are we there yet" questions and "he's touching me" complaints.

My obsession with arriving at our destination with as few stops as possible means that snacks and lunches are prepacked for each child in an insulated lunch box filled with sandwiches and string cheese and the car is loaded with snacks and mini water bottles. The boys have access to their food and can eat on their timetable, and I keep a bag of sandwiches and crackers up front with me.

Yet traveling with three little boys has its challenges. My youngest no longer wants to go into the women's bathroom with me, even though he's at that age where I could probably still get away with it. However, the men's bathroom is the one place they can toss water or lob wet paper towels at one another's heads without my watchful eye.

At one particularly inopportune moment, I was forced to pull over at the closest stop, which happened to be a not-very-nice rest area. I can't explain it but something in my spirit told me not to separate myself from my kids. Family restrooms used to be a blessing when they were younger but preteen sons are no longer comfortable being in the bathroom with their mommy. However, this was one time I chose to trust my gut over my kids' discomfort and I locked us all in the bigger bathroom.

I turned around, closed my eyes, and gave the boys as much privacy as I could. Then I made them do the same for me. We washed our hands and hightailed it back to the van as I prayed for God's protection. I don't know if anything would have happened had I let the boys go into the men's bathroom, but sometimes we have to trust our instincts.

This is why prayer is so important. Before we pull out of the driveway, gas station, or rest area, someone offers a prayer for traveling mercies. We ask God for safety, to protect us and the car, and I add, "Please, God, keep us invisible to those who wish to do us harm."

I'm so grateful for the modern advancements in travel we enjoy today. Mary and Joseph traveled to the temple when Jesus was twelve years old. There were no rest stops or drive-throughs. The journey was long, dusty, and hot . . . not one I'd like to experience. On the way home, Mary and Joseph realized Jesus wasn't with the group. Scripture says they didn't find Jesus until the third day. Can you imagine?

I've lost my children momentarily in a crowd and it's the most frightening feeling in the entire world.

Jesus's response to Mary was that He was doing the will of His Father. Now, if my kids said that to me, we'd have some issues, but Mary knew Jesus was God's Son and she knew that He *was* doing the will of God the Father.

We long to keep our kids safe and sound but there is a time when they will leave us and go on road trips of their own. It's our job to prepare them to be able to do just that.

Michelle's Intel

Road trips can be so fun, but they can also be the worst thing ever! And, really, the only difference between the two is your attitude. Once the girls grew out of the "Abby is on my side of the car!" and "Ally is breathing my air" phase, road trips became a fun adventure, and the chance to make new memories with every mile.

There's something freeing about a road trip. You get to eat snacks on the road you wouldn't normally eat because you're counting carbs. You get to listen to inspiring podcasts you normally wouldn't take the time to hear. You get to play road games; our favorite is still Slug Bug, lol. And you get to act silly at every rest stop, because, after all, no one knows you!

One such rest stop lives in the Adams Family Funny files. The girls and I ran to the little girls room, and as I was washing my hands, Kelly Clarkson's song "Walk Away" started playing, and I just couldn't help myself. Maybe it was being restrained in a seat belt for so many hours, but I could not stop myself from dancing. And I mean, I got my groove on! Facial expressions and everything.

When Ally and Abby exited their stalls, they joined in the dancefest while washing their hands. Just as we were butt bumping our best butt bumps, an older woman exited another stall and glared at us like we were completely insane. We calmly walked toward the door and laughed the next thirty miles.

Road trips, and most of life's moments, are what you make them, so make them memorable.

God Calls Me to Let Him Lead

We need to prepare for our life's journey just like we do for a road trip. The Bible says that God makes a path for us. "You gave a wide place for my steps under me, and my feet did not slip" (Ps. 18:36 ESV). Just like we trust Him to keep us safe, we have to be open and ready for the road He calls us to walk.

Things to Pack on a Road Trip

- Paper towels
- Wipes
- Bottles of water
- Snacks
- Phone chargers
- Easy access to a change of clothes
- Cash and change for unexpected tolls
- Activities for the kids
- Tissues
- Plastic bags for trash (or vomit)
- Ginger chews or ginger ale (a great "cure" for motion sickness)

18

They Call Me Rainbow Recorder

Michelle's Intel

Rainbows have always meant a lot to our family. On the day that my sweet father went to heaven, we left the rehabilitation center where Daddy had died, and as we headed home, a double rainbow stretched over the highway between Decatur and Fort Worth, Texas.

It was as if God were saying, "I've got your daddy, and this is your promise that you'll see him again someday." Just as I was processing the beautiful display of God's promise to me, Abby said, "God put two rainbows in the sky just for us—one for me and one for Ally because He knew how much we would miss Papaw."

Precious.

Both girls had also grabbed on to that promise, giving them the same comfort I was experiencing from gazing at the wash of color across the morning sky.

Since then, it seems any time we have a big decision to make or a situation where we really need the love of our heavenly Father, a comforting arch of color will appear out of nowhere. It's just like a hug from heaven.

For example, when we first moved Allyson to Los Angeles to attend the Fashion Institute of Design & Merchandising, I was one distressed mama.

While I was thrilled that Ally was following her dream and pursuing a career in fashion, I couldn't believe I was going to have to leave my baby girl in LA all by herself, two thousand miles from home.

We had prayed over her move, and God had shown us great favor at every turn; still, I was nervous and upset.

She is only eighteen! I thought. *How is she going to survive in this huge city?*

And what if we've chosen the wrong apartment complex for her? . . . What if it's unsafe? Maybe we should move her closer to school . . . Will she be able to navigate the public transportation system? It's so confusing and she gets lost so easily . . .

The LA weather seemed to match my mood that afternoon—rainy and dreary. I was lost in worry when all of a sudden, my eyes shifted upward.

Painted across the gray sky was an absolutely beautiful rainbow, stretching right over the top of the apartment building that would be Ally's new home.

Overcome with emotion, I couldn't speak so I just pointed. We all took a moment to gaze at God's goodness; His promise that everything was going to be okay.

Ally and I locked eyes and exchanged knowing smiles.

It was exactly what I needed before I could leave my baby girl and head back home.

Over the years, Abby and Ally have texted Jeff and me dozens of rainbow pictures, sharing the corresponding testimonies—because there's always an accompanying story. Of course, as a writer I must document each one—taking a picture and recording the testimony.

I'm sure there are other families who have "rainbow moments" just like us, but each time we behold a glorious rainbow, it seems like God colored the sky just for us. Each rainbow of reassurance has brought us closer together as a family and caused our faith to grow a little more.

Time after time, God has shown His love in such a personal way. Sometimes it's through rainbows in the sky; other times, through a Scripture passage that jumps off the page; still other times through a kind word from a stranger. He is so faithful! God knows just what we need, exactly when we need it.

As moms, there are going to be days we need all of the rainbows of reassurance we can get—can I hear an amen? But isn't it great to know that while we're worrying, God is working?

All we have to do is trust in Him and look up, and train our children to do the same.

Bethany's JETTliner

The week before my incredible grandma died, dimes started appearing out of nowhere in the strangest places. Finding loose change is nothing new, but finding a single dime repeatedly was unusual. After finding the third dime, I recalled a story my aunt told me. Dimes were an inside joke with her and my papaw, and after he died, she found dimes in unlikely places, like in the corner of her shower.

She lived alone.

The dimes were reminders from heaven that he was looking down on her. When I started finding dimes, I felt the same, and started photographing them and texting the evidence to my mom and aunt.

After our first military move to Biloxi, our dryer broke. Justin and

I scoured Facebook Marketplace and Craigslist for a used one. Serendipitously, a woman messaged me in the military wives Facebook group page. She had an old rusted dryer that was broken so she was happy to give it to us for free.

Better yet, she lived one street over.

Free sounded great to me, plus Justin is Mr. Fix-It, so our husbands coordinated the delivery. Within the hour, Justin had bought the necessary part, fixed the dryer, and I was ready to clean some clothes. Except the dryer kept making this strange noise. I checked the lint trap and felt around on the inside but couldn't figure out what caused the clanging.

My handy hubby got out his tools and took the dryer apart. After fifteen minutes, he came into the kitchen, took the dish towel from my hand, and opened his palm.

There sat the most worn-down dime I'd ever seen. It was barely recognizable. And all I could think was that God was giving me comfort with a dime from a woman I'd met randomly on Facebook who lived one street over and blessed us with that free ugly dryer.

God is an amazingly cool God. The dimes may be just dimes and random coincidence, but I believe that sometimes He provides tangible ways to show us that He loves us. Those dimes send warm fuzzies to my heart but I don't let it stop there. Each dime is a reminder to thank Him for my grandparents' lives and examples, to pray specifically for my aunt and my family, and to thank Him for always being with me even when I didn't feel it.

God Calls Me to Believe

Genesis 9:13 says, "I have placed my rainbow in the clouds. It is the sign of my covenant with you and with all the earth" (NLT). Even on the days when you can't find the physical rainbow, you can still trust God to perform His Word in your life and in the lives of your children. Be expectant. Be looking for the rainbows. And don't forget to praise Him when He comes through.

Record the Rainbow Moments in Your Family

If you're like most moms, you're the family memory preserver via picture taking, scrapbooking, and storytelling. Well, since you're probably already fulfilling that role, why not encourage your kiddos to share their very own "rainbow moments" with you once a week, and you can record them in a special journal? Then, like David in the Bible, you can read back through them, rehearse the victories, and praise Him for His faithfulness.

19

They Call Me Thrifty

Bethany's JETTliner

Who doesn't love a good bargain?

A few years ago, our family was a yard sale-ing machine. On Friday nights I perused Craigslist for the next day's yard sales, and on Saturday mornings the Jett family piled into the minivan to score some gently used merchandise. After hitting a few houses, we'd run into McDonald's, use the facilities, and grab some one-dollar sausage burritos for the kids and coffees for us parents.

Some of our best garage sale finds were a set of women's golf clubs for eight dollars, a green faux-snakeskin travel bag for eight dollars that works perfectly for when I travel to conferences, and my husband's favorite win: a video game called Portal 2 that he bought for five dollars, played, sent to his brother who also played, then traded in for a twenty-one dollar credit at the video game store.

With three growing and often messy boys, there is a lot less stress over ripped pant knees from their practice sliding across the carpet when their pants cost less than a Happy Meal. In one spectacular find, a mom was cleaning out her son's closet and I scored ten pairs of name-brand quality shorts that lasted through all three of my boys and were in great shape when I passed them on to a friend for her little boys.

Along with yard sales, Justin and I love thrift stores. I found an artificial Christmas tree on display at Goodwill and we decorated it for eight years before giving it to a friend who had never owned a Christmas tree.

Even though I have tons of jewelry from my direct sales days, my favorite necklace and earrings came from the two-dollar bin at Plato's Closet, and don't get me started on all the designer shoes I've found there. Michelle and I share a love of thrift stores and yard sales and often find each other supercool tops during our individual shopping trips.

Along with shopping at thrift stores, I've taught myself to cut my boys' hair. At fourteen dollars a pop times three boys, I'd rather save that forty-five dollars every couple of months. YouTube has been a fantastic resource and if I mess up badly I can shave their heads and try again next time.

When Justin was stationed at an Air Force base in Mississippi, we learned about a wonderful organization called Airman's Attic. Military members can donate clothes and household goods, including furniture. The only service members who benefit from these donations are ranked E-5 or lower. The boys and I took advantage of the books we found there, and after reading them, brought them back for other families to enjoy.

Saving money on gently used items lets you splurge on other things. For me, it's a trip to the salon every five to six weeks and certain brands of makeup. For you it might be something totally different. Either way, you save the difference when you don't buy at retail price.

Not only do we shop at yard sales, but we've also hosted several of our own. My husband loves to declutter and purge our possessions. Hosting yard sales teaches our kids to let go of their possessions. They earn some cash and we treat them to a special lunch once the yard is cleaned up and the sale is over. One time we let the boys set up our Keurig, and they sold coffee and donuts to the early-morning buyers.

We're teaching our children to not get addicted to their things. Luke 12:15 says, "Then he said, 'Beware! Guard against every kind of greed. Life is not measured by how much you own'" (NLT). My husband and I can be a bit snobby with certain material goods, aka all things Apple. One of the reasons we love to go to yard sales and thrift stores is because it reminds me that these are just items and I want my kids to see that things still have use even if they aren't brand-new.

The thought of my children becoming materialistic is a concern of mine, so I use these opportunities to differentiate between spending money on items that should be brand-new or brand name, and recognizing the items that will save you money by buying used or generic.

I love to decorate my home with pretty things, and I value well-made, high-quality clothing and accessories. However, I have to guard my own heart against making purchases that don't help my family's bottom line. Since we're saving to buy a home, I'm using up all my skin-care samples and purchasing less expensive cleansers until we're at a point where the high-end products are easier on the checkbook. By mixing in thrift-store and yard-sale finds, not only does it help keep me in check, but it also provides a good example to my boys that things are just things.

The key is that by being wise with our money, we can use the savings from buying used to help others or even purchase the things we want to buy new.

Michelle's Intel

I love that my girls are Goodwill, thrift-store, consignment-boutique, and yard-sale shoppers. Both Jeff and I love a good sale, and though we always have nice things, it literally hurts my soul to pay full price for anything. We have managed to take bargain shopping to a whole new level over the years.

When my girls were preteens, they were a little embarrassed to say their designer purse came from a consignment store, but today, they proudly announce it! Our family loves sharing online yard-sale finds and going on flea market road trips together.

So. Much. Fun.

Now that my daughters are married and decorating homes of their own, while staying within their household budgets, I love hearing about all the ReStore furniture they've beautifully refurbished, or the perfect mirror they bought at a yard sale for two dollars, repainted, and used in their guest bathroom.

It makes me so proud to watch my girls be good stewards of the money and talents God gave them.

With all of the DIY YouTube tutorials, Pinterest pages, and HGTV shows, we can literally transform trash finds into treasured pieces, and there's such a sense of accomplishment when we do so.

Abby and her husband, Micah, have taken budget-mindedness to a whole new level. They practice Dave Ramsey's proven program of paying off debt and building wealth. Jeff and I marvel at their commitment to being debt-free and we applaud them for being great stewards. It sure does this mama's heart good to know that both of my girls are better with money than I have ever been.

I say, thrifty moms unite! Listen, I'd write more but I'm meeting someone to pick up a deal I made on Bedford Online Yard Sale—no kidding.

God Calls Me Valuable

While we sometimes think our worth is determined by our possessions, God says that we are worth more to Him than rubies (Prov. 31:10).

Additionally, we are so valuable to God that He literally knows the number of hairs on our head (Luke 12:6–7). Considering my hair sheds all over the place, that number changes on the daily.

No matter how much money we have in this life, let's store our riches in heaven where treasure lasts forever in God's economy.

Ways to Teach Money Lessons

1. Assign age-appropriate chores so they can earn some money.

2. Teach them to save and give instead of spending all their money at once.

3. Challenge them to see how many clothing items they can buy for ten or twenty dollars at a thrift store.

4. Offer to match their savings up to a certain dollar amount for higher-priced items that take longer to save to buy.

5. Give your kids a set amount of money and have them make the grocery-shopping decisions for dinner.

Bonus: With tweens or teens, let them keep half the money they bring back after an outing. If you give them twenty dollars to cover meals and souvenirs and they bring back eight dollars, you get four dollars and they keep four dollars. The caveat is that all the receipts have to be brought back to ensure your child didn't skip meals in order to pocket extra cash.[6]

---

6. A big thanks to the Tedesco family for modeling this with their daughters when we were in youth ministry.

20

They Call Me Supersleuth

Michelle's Intel

I'm pretty sure Abby and Ally thought I worked for the FBI when they were growing up because no matter how clever their story or how convincing their delivery, I always found out the truth—usually before they were even back home.

Now, don't get me wrong. They were good girls most of the time, but certainly not all of the time.

This incident fell into the latter category.

Abby had been planning a movie night with her group of friends all week. Finally, Friday had arrived and she was super excited.

"What're you guys going to see?" I asked my then fourteen-year-old.

"We don't know yet," she answered, grabbing her coat. "There are a couple of good ones playing within fifteen minutes of each other. We'll decide once we get there."

Translation: *We'll see whichever movie all the cute guys are going to, and then we'll also go to that movie.*

"Just as long as none of the choices are rated R," I said, shooting her my "I mean business" look.

"I know, Mom." She groaned. "Tara's here. I'm leaving!"

"Have a great time," I called after her.

Later as Jeff and I were heading to bed, Abby and her best friend arrived home, raided the fridge, and headed for Abby's bedroom.

"Night, Mom," Abby called from the other side of the house.

"Hey, Ab, what'd you guys end up seeing?"

"*Last Holiday*."

"With Queen Latifah?" I asked. "I've been wanting to see that."

"Yep, really good . . . Night!"

With that, Abby closed her door and I closed ours.

I never gave it another thought until later that week when I was doing laundry. Having learned to empty all pockets after the pink lip gloss incident of 2004, I went through Abby's jeans pockets and discovered Chapstick, two dollars, and a movie ticket stub. Just as I was about to throw away the ticket stub, I felt the Holy Spirit nudging me to look at it.

So I did.

Expecting to see *Last Holiday* printed on the stub, imagine my surprise when it read: *Underworld: Evolution*—rated R.

My first instinct was to ground her until the return of Jesus, but my second instinct was to use my supersleuthing skills to find out if she would come clean when questioned. I planned to push a little that afternoon.

But I didn't have to; Ab came to me first.

She confessed that she'd lied about going to see *Last Holiday* and that she was really sorry. And she confirmed what I already knew—she went to the R-rated movie because all of her friends, including the boy she liked, went to that one. But she also confirmed something else I knew—Ab was a good girl who had simply made a bad decision.

I was glad my supersleuthing ways had proven successful, and I was also glad I could show mercy to my fourteen-year-old who already felt bad enough. As moms, we are innate detectives, which serves us well (especially during our children's teen years) but oftentimes, our investigative ways uncover our children's bad behavior and big old blunders. When that happens, if you're like me, you sometimes wish you hadn't been such a great detective because it's hard to put on the disciplinarian hat and deal with whatever you've uncovered.

Mom to mom, let me urge you to choose your battles. I'm not saying be a pushover, but I am saying it's a good thing to show mercy. After all, haven't we all made a bad decision on occasion? My youngest daughter, Ally, coined the term "accidentally bad" when she got into trouble as a little girl, and it still makes me smile to this day because we're all "accidentally bad" from time to time. I'm so thankful our heavenly Father gives us new mercies every morning, aren't you?

I'm not turning in my supersleuth badge anytime soon, and you shouldn't either, but I am suggesting we ask God to help us use those supersleuthing abilities to find ways to discipline with mercy and parent in such a way that our children aren't afraid to tell us about their "accidentally bad" days.

Bethany's JETTliner

My oldest child and I are having a doozy of a time with "nonaccidental behavior" such as truth-telling and brother-bullying and anything else that an oldest child does when trying to distance himself from younger siblings. The hormones are kicking in during these "I'm almost a teenager" days and he's learning to assert his independence while battling the simultaneous need to still be a kid.

Some days I don't even know what to do. I literally #canteven. And when things come to a head and there are tears all around, I know my son—who is so much the spitting image *and* personality of his daddy— also has a lot of my personality. We're both people-pleasing overachievers who punish ourselves better than anyone else could. And since I see this in my son, I want to help him not guilt himself to the point where he's depressed.

After our last episode when his choices got his younger brothers in trouble, he was particularly crushed with guilt. I spent thirty minutes dealing with the aftermath of the punishment. By the time I left the younger two, my oldest couldn't stop the flow of tears. We talked about the consequences of our actions and how sin can hurt us and other people.

Then on the dry-erase board above his bed, I wrote the words "God's mercies are new *every* morning. God's love never changes." I made him repeat this several times before kissing him goodnight.

It's been over a month, and my son hasn't erased those words. I want him to know that no matter how bad the day is, God loves him, I love him, and no matter how badly today sucks, tomorrow is a new day with no mistakes.

God Calls Me Mercy Receiver

Lamentations 3:22–23 says, "The steadfast love of the LORD never ceases; his mercies never come to an end; they are new every morning" (ESV). I'm so glad God never runs out of mercy, and I'm so thankful He isn't keeping a score sheet up in heaven, tallying up all of my "accidentally bad" days. How about you? Hebrews 8:12 says, "For I will be merciful toward their iniquities, and I will remember their sins no more" (ESV). Meditate on that blessing today and try not to be "accidentally bad." And even when you do have a bad day, praise God for His grace and then offer that same grace to your kiddos.

Three Tips to Get Your Kids Talking

Of course, we're master detectives because we're moms, but wouldn't it be nice if we didn't have to use our supersleuthing skills all the time to get information out of our children? Wouldn't it be amazing if they talked to us about what's bothering them?

While there are phases when our kiddos probably won't be as conversational simply because of their age, here are three tips from various parenting experts to help you better communicate with your children:

- *Be specific when you ask questions:* Instead of asking, "How was your day?" and getting the typical "Fine" answer, ask, "What did you like better today—snack time or recess?" That specific question is more likely to get your little one chatting about the day.

- *Multitask and ask:* This seems to work especially well for tweens and teens. Rather than cornering your teenage daughter in her room, asking her about the slumber party last night (that you heard via another mom had resulted in lots of hurt feelings), suggest the two of you take a walk. Then, once you've hit the trail and the endorphins are firing, casually talk about anything she wants to discuss. This time will more than likely lead to talk of the slumber party.

- *Get on their level:* With your toddlers and preschoolers, this will be floor time. If they're playing blocks or coloring, get on your tummy next to them and engage. While you're building a block mansion or coloring a masterpiece, talk about "stuff." With you on their level, it's less scary and more natural for your little ones to share with you.

In dealing with teens, this might mean piling on the couch together to watch your favorite recorded shows. Then, in between popcorn munching and bathroom breaks, use this nonthreatening time to chat about the day. If there's something bothering your teenage daughter, this may be the time she feels most comfortable bringing it up. You're both looking at the TV so there's no eye contact, which also makes it easier to share information that leaves her feeling vulnerable.

21

They Call Me "by Myself"

Bethany's JETTliner

Single parenting is not for the faint of heart.

I tasted the burden of having every decision, every punishment, every need, every obligation fall on my shoulders when Justin deployed overseas. I became both parents to my kids, and there was no one to pick up my slack when I inevitably dropped the ball.

My boys are sweethearts, but kids have this sixth sense for when their parents are at their breaking point, and they definitely use it to their advantage. Many days I did laundry at eleven at night and then worked until three in the morning just to get up three hours later to start the day.

Some days I don't want to do everything by myself but some days I have to.

I didn't have a routine as the sole caregiver, and it took time to develop my rhythm. There were countless times when I needed a break and ordinarily would have excused myself to my room for a little while.

With no other adult in the house, those quiet moments didn't happen until the boys were asleep.

During this time, my mom lived about six minutes down the road from us. Each week she invited one of the boys to stay overnight at her apartment. I don't know why, but it didn't matter which two kids stayed behind—the fighting and bickering ceased, and the house was more calm. Once the three were together again, it was chaos.

I've never felt more alone than during those first few months. I had to be strong for my kids who mourned their daddy's absence, and I had to calm the night terrors when my boys dreamed of their father being beheaded by ISIS.

The small circle of those "in the know" checked in on me and kept us in their prayers, and the support of the other military spouses helped me hang in there. I wasn't the first military wife to go through a deployment and I know it won't be our last.

Six months of being a single mom is nothing compared to moms who live this reality every single day for years on end. Your job is even tougher because you are the sole support of your family. That is a burden I wish you didn't have to bear.

You are a hero to your kids, and you're a hero to me. I can't compare my experience to yours because mine ended after only a few months. However, I empathize to the max because the exhaustion from single parenting is big and the stress is heavy.

Yet every mom can relate to a certain extent. We all have times when we are dangling at the end of our rope with a chasm underneath us, and no help in sight.

When my mental, spiritual, and physical strength were depleted, I could only turn to God. His Word says, "And my God will supply every need of yours according to his riches in glory in Christ Jesus" (Phil. 4:19 ESV).

Moms can have a confidence and strength that is a testimony to their kids. It is God's strength in us that allows us to dig deeper than we ever knew.

God's Word is a source of strength and support systems are vital. In the same way we need to rely on Jesus, we also need to rely on people. I don't know what I would have done without the people around me. It was during this deployment that I found what is now our home church and, because we homeschooled for part of the deployment, our co-op was also a support system.

Michelle's Intel

As if it weren't hard enough that my sweet mama was fighting cancer, I had to go through it all without my husband. The girls and I had already moved to Indiana where my mom was living so that I could help with her caregiving, and so that the girls could spend as much time with their mamaw as possible. Meanwhile, Jeff stayed behind in Texas to continue working and trying to sell our home.

Days turned to weeks and weeks turned to months—still our Texas home wouldn't sell. I had never before been both mom and dad to our girls, and I was completely overwhelmed. Abby and Ally were in middle school during this season, and they were sassy. But they were also hurting, trying to adjust to a new school thousands of miles from their friends, as well as dealing with Mamaw's illness, so I cut them some slack. Sometimes too much.

I was on two book deadlines at the time, coaching cheerleading, going to every parent-teacher obligation, helping with homework, taking care of the household chores, doing laundry offsite because our rental house didn't have a washer and dryer, and trying to redo the girls' bedrooms so it felt more like home.

And I was failing miserably at all of it.

Just when I thought things couldn't get any worse, I took my girls to a local high school football game one Friday night for some fun, which we'd been lacking, and I overheard someone in the bleachers gossiping. This guy, who had to be the world's loudest whisperer, said, "I heard she left her husband, took the kids, and filed for divorce . . . She probably has a boyfriend."

Really?

It's a good thing I was "prayed up" that night, or Mr. Loud Whisperer would've been very sorry he ever opened his mouth. Rather than confront him, I simply stood up, walked to the bathroom, and cried for half an hour.

To say it was a difficult season is the biggest understatement ever.

I only had to endure my single parent status eight months, but those were the longest eight months of my life. I say all of that to say this—I salute you, brave single moms. I am in awe of what you are able to do, and I respect you very much. I also pray for you—I pray that you have peace in your decisions and support from extended family and friends. And I pray that you know how awesome you are, and that you feel the Lord's arms wrapped around you today.

You. Are. Amazing.

And for all of us, here's the thing. Whenever you're feeling down, overwhelmed, and scared, the devil will always add insult to injury. He loves to kick a mama when she's down.

So keep an eye out for Satan whispering to you (that you're a failure, that God doesn't love you) and call those statements what they are—absolute, complete, and total lies.

Whether you're a single mama all the time, or you're alone in your parenting for just a season, remember this—you are not alone. Your heavenly Father promises to never leave you, so lean on Him. The Word says

He will be a husband to the husbandless and a Father to the fatherless, so claim those verses as your own and move forward with the courage and capability that's already in you.

God Calls Me Perfect in Weakness

A verse that I repeated to myself on the daily during Justin's absence was 2 Corinthians 12:9: "My grace is sufficient for you, for my power is made perfect in weakness." Heaven knows I was weak and struggling at times, but God is glorified when we are at our weakest. There is comfort in knowing that God is with you and will see you through: "The one who calls you is faithful, and he will do it" (1 Thess. 5:24). My sweet sister in Christ, you are enough. God has you and He will never let you fall.

Ways to Find Support Systems

There are many reasons why we find ourselves as single parents, whether it be for a few days, a few months, many years, or a lifetime. No matter our circumstances, we can rely on a loving God who is with us every step of the way. Support systems, be it in-person or online, can be lifesavers. When you find a friend (at church, your kids' school, work, your workout class, book club, or wherever) you can vent and cry to, hold on to her tight. Parenting is not easy, and when every decision is on your shoulders, quite frankly it's overwhelming. Let's support each other and cheer each other on. After all, it's in all of our hearts to be the best moms for our babies and by God's grace, we are.

22

They Call Me Supporter

Michelle's Intel

My cell phone was blowing up with texts from my younger daughter, Allyson. I could literally "hear" the fear woven into each text.

Ally, in her final semester of college in California, was experiencing the panic that many college seniors go through.

Remember that season?

You've worked ridiculously hard to get into your college of choice; you've studied many hours to make good grades; and suddenly, it's your final semester and you have to keep your grades up while preparing your résumé and portfolio so you can begin your job search.

She was simply overwhelmed.

I was typing responses as quickly as I could when my phone rang.

It was Ally; she was sobbing.

"I don't know what I'm going to do," Ally confessed. "If I stay in LA, I'll have to get like three jobs to support myself . . . and who knows if my internship will actually turn into a full-time position? And if I move back to the Midwest, there aren't that many fashion design positions so I'd probably just end up working retail. And you don't need a college degree to work retail. I feel lost, Mom."

I tried to reassure her that God had a plan, that He wouldn't have called her to the Fashion Institute of Design & Merchandising in LA to leave her stranded and without a job. I quoted several encouraging Scriptures and reassured her: "God's got this, Al."

"I know," she said. "I just wish He'd give me a sign or something."

I knew what she meant. It would be so nice if God gave us clear signs when we need them. You know, maybe write our answer in the sky or send an angel with a special message from heaven . . . something along those lines. But that wouldn't take much faith, would it? Instead, I said what any spiritual support system would say: "We don't need a sign, Ally. We have His Word. That's all you need."

She calmed down a bit and we said our goodbyes, but the Mama Bear in me wanted to start taking care of business for my youngest. I wanted to comb the job search websites and send her every position I thought she was qualified for and then come up with a Plan B if none of those jobs panned out. I had just started to research headhunters in her field when I heard that gentle voice whisper, "I've got this."

I knew His voice, and I understood my role—do nothing. You see, if we try to solve all of our adult children's problems, then we rob them of experiencing God coming through for them in a big way. We eliminate the need for them to trust God and walk out their journey of faith. It seems the apron strings had stretched from Indiana to Los Angeles and it was time to cut them and simply be her supporter, not her savior. She already had one of those.

Later that night, Ally sent me a picture text of her devotional that day. It read: "Approach this day with awareness of Who is Boss. . . . Don't try to figure out what is happening. Simply trust Me."

And the Scripture for that day? Jeremiah 29:11—Ally's life verse.

I texted back, "There's your sign. :)"

I love it when God shows Himself big in our children's lives, don't you? That day Ally and I both learned a lesson. She learned she could rely on her heavenly Father because, after all, I won't always be around, but He will. And I learned that I can trust God to take care of my babies no matter how old they are. I also learned that the role of supporter and spiritual advisor is a blessing with boundaries. All I needed to do that day, and all I will ever need to do where my children are concerned, is pray for them, encourage them, support them, listen to them, and let God do His thing in their lives. That's a supporting role I'm happy to accept.

Bethany's JETTliner

Remember the terrible twos and the even more terrible threes? That stage of independence was an absolute trial with my boys. Everything took longer because they had to do it themselves. I could put their shorts on them in two seconds, but no. "I do it" became the cry, and my brazen babies would push my hands away and throw a temper tantrum if they weren't allowed to dress themselves.

Interestingly, my kids always knew when we were in a hurry because that's when their need to "I do it" was strongest.

God created our kids to be independent of us. At some point we have to let them go, and the loosening of those Mommy-will-do-it strands starts way too early. I want to do things for my kids. Making them a big breakfast and hearing their appreciative murmurs as they fill their bellies satisfies a part of me that I don't even know how to describe.

Sometimes it can be hard to know when to let our kids learn on their own.

And sometimes your kids will let you know.

"Mommy and Daddy, remember when you said we could ask you anything?"

My heart pounded so fast. Was this the dreaded "where do babies come from" question?

Justin and I looked at each other with wide-eyed expressions.

"Yeeeeeeeessssssssss," I said.

"Will you teach me how to learn to use the stove?"

Can you hear the sigh of relief?

I love taking care of my kids, but one of my jobs is to teach them to take care of themselves. So lately the boys have started making dinner and cracking the eggs into the bowl under my watchful no-shells-in-the-omelet-please eye.

And when the shells make it into the eggs, or the pizza gets burned, or the water boils over, it's my job to teach them how to recover so they know that I'll be here to catch them when they fall.

God Calls Me to Be Still

Psalm 46:10 says, "Be still, and know that I am God." Sometimes, that's all we need to do—simply be still and watch God work. Obviously, when our children are little they require much more attention and guidance, but as they get older, we need to let God be God in their lives.

Three Ways to Help Without Helping

It's funny. When I teach my college course, Writing for Children, I always share this tip: "Let your main character—the child—solve the problem in the story. Don't let Pastor Rick sweep in and save the day because Pastor Rick won't always be there in real life. We want to show the child in the story as the problem-solver and hero. That empowers the reader to think, *Yes, I can do that too!"*

You'd think if I teach that concept when writing for kids, I'd have an easier time implementing it when raising kids . . . not so much. It's hard to let go and let God, isn't it? Well, here are three ways to help without helping.

- *Let your child know you're available:* In other words, don't try to do everything for your child but let your kiddo know that if he or she tries and fails, you're there to help.

- *Encourage your child:* Let your child know you think he or she is amazing and can accomplish the task at hand. Sometimes, that's all your kiddo needs to succeed—just a voice of affirmation.

- *Share your victories and failures:* It's good to be transparent with your children. Let them celebrate your victories with you, but also let them know you don't always get it right. Let them see you learn from your failed attempts to achieve a goal so they can do the same.

23

They Call Me Housekeeper (Sometimes)

Bethany's JETTliner

My kids pee in the bathroom.

Let me be more specific. My kids pee in the bath*tub*.

Let me be more precise. My kids pee in the bathtub *for fun*.

We live in a townhouse with two-and-a-half bathrooms: one for the boys, one for Justin and me, and one downstairs for guests. However, when company comes to stay, the boys' bathroom becomes the guest bathroom and the instructions to my children are clear: You may use Mommy and Daddy's bathroom, but do not, under any circumstances, use the newly appointed guest bathroom.

For any reason.

But during one guest's stay, my boys chose not to use my bathroom for all their potty needs. Instead, my little boys peed in the guest bathtub *without rinsing it afterward* and also dropped their poopy drawers on the tile floor *and left them there.*

W-h-a-t?

Since I was staying out of that bathroom during my friend's stay, I didn't know about any of this.

My friend didn't tell me about the stinky pants and smelly tub for a couple of days. Mortified doesn't begin to cover how I felt.

I never expected to be monitoring bathroom issues for my children after the diaper days ended.

Now my boys are in charge of cleaning the bathrooms, specifically the toilets, and any underwear streaked from unwiped booties gets thrown away immediately. After I tossed several pairs, the guilty party is now responsible for paying for his new underpants.

Mama. Ain't. Having. That. Nonsense.

When Justin was deployed, all the housework fell on my shoulders so the boys kicked in some elbow grease. My youngest oversees the laundry and the older two boys switch off with the kitchen duties and straightening the living room. Justin and I tackle the bigger jobs but the boys are responsible for their stations . . . and they don't get paid for it. These are the jobs they do because they live here and because the mess is usually theirs.

Justin's love language is acts of service. After many years of in-depth research, I've learned that the man I love with all my heart doesn't care so much if the laundry is piling over or if the bathroom counter is covered in cosmetics. He cares about what he sees when he first walks into the house.

We call this "the eyeline."

The boys stand at the front door and gaze around the house at all the clutter, trash, toys, papers, dishes, and so forth that need to be picked up, tossed out, or taken care of. On the count of three, they race to make it shine. I've dubbed this standard "Mommy Perfect," mostly to connect the words *mommy* and *perfect* in their minds (heh heh heh), but also to show them what I expect of them.

"This house should look better than a hotel room" is another phrase I say.

I want our home to be in a constant state of lived-in respectability so that a guest could drop by at any time and I wouldn't be freaking out if there is an unflushed potty or last night's dinner remnants on the stovetop.

I've often said that my home is a direct result of how cluttered my brain is. When I'm on deadline and I feel chaotic, it shows. When I feel calm, my house is calm and kept-together. There doesn't seem to be much in-between. As I write this, my suitcases are sitting at the foot of our bed, unpacked from last week's conference. I leave in two days for another conference so at least my husband won't have to walk around my luggage once I'm gone.

Psalm 51:10 says, "Create in me a clean heart, O God, and renew a right spirit within me" (ESV). The state of my heart can often be witnessed in the state of my home.

A clean home cultivates productivity.

A clean heart cultivates righteousness.

Staying on top of the household chores is a drag but I love the result. Thirty minutes of cleaning can save hours of frustration because items are in their place and minutes aren't lost looking for things.

Marie Kondo's *The Life-Changing Magic of Tidying Up* was a game changer for us. Now that we've moved and haven't had a yard sale in a while, belongings are starting to pile up. I need to review her strategies and implement another cleaning day. Honestly, following her steps allowed us to maintain a super clean house with three little boys in just minutes a day.

Truth be told, cleaning is the worst and supervising my children's cleaning is life-sucking, but the goal is that by the time the boys are grown and out of my house, they'll know how to take care of their things, do their own laundry, and run a household. To my future daughters-in-law, you're welcome.

Michelle's Intel

Hi, I'm Michelle, and I'm a recovering neat freak.

It's funny; when I was a kid growing up, my mom said she worried I'd be a slob all my life. My room was never dirty, but it was always disorganized. It drove her crazy! I didn't mind too much because I was rarely in my room. Once I was ready for the day, I was gone until bedtime most days.

But once I married and had a house of my own, everything changed for me. (Okay, not everything. I still have a junk drawer in every room.)

I wanted lines in the carpeting from a freshly vacuumed room. I wanted shiny countertops. I wanted all the clothes put away the minute laundry was done. And if I found a dish in the sink, I had a mini meltdown. My house, at all times, was picture perfect, and I took great pride in that fact.

Then . . . children happened.

One right after the other.

I tried to keep a perfect house for a while. I really did. But one day it hit me—I'm spending all my hours after I get home from work picking up and cleaning, and I'm not even enjoying my girls or my adorable husband.

Something had to give . . . and it was me. I gave up on perfection and settled for "pretty good."

I also allowed Jeff to once again help me around the house. Always before, he couldn't do any household task to please me, so he quit helping. Big mistake on my part. Huge! Once we started tag-teaming the laundry, the vacuuming, the kitchen mess, and the dusting, the household chores weren't nearly as time-consuming, which left us time to just "be" and enjoy some much-needed family time.

If you're a neat freak, take a note from a recovering neat freak: life is too short to stress about a dish or two in the sink. You'll get to it, but never let your household chores take precedence over your family.

God Calls Me to Manage My Household

Keeping a clean house is a good thing, but I often like to put it off to do what I consider *better* things. When Jesus visited Mary and Martha, Martha obsessed about the housekeeping and hostessing while Mary sat at Jesus's feet. Jesus said, "Martha, Martha, you are anxious and troubled about many things, but one thing is necessary. Mary has chosen the good portion, which will not be taken away from her" (Luke 10:41–42 ESV).

I wish that reading a book or working on my business and schoolwork were "the good portion." However, I appreciate that Jesus isn't worried about those tasks. Do they need to get done? Sure, but if we become obsessive, we can place being a "neat freak" onto a pedestal where it doesn't belong.

Tips for an Organized Home

- Don't be afraid to throw things away. We hoard items in our junk drawer "just in case we need them." We rarely need them. Now we say, "If I need this item that costs thirty cents, I'll just go buy it" and drop it in the trash.

- Keep a bin or tote purely for donations. If I pull something out of my closet that I don't wear or out of my kids' drawers that doesn't fit, I can toss it into the giveaway tote. When it's full, items can be sold on Craigslist or Facebook Marketplace, or donated to the thrift store or church.

- Read Marie Kondo's *The Life-Changing Magic of Tidying Up* or catch her show *Tidying Up* on Netflix. Following these principles changed our lives!

24

They Call Me Holiday Planner Extraordinaire

Michelle's Intel

Yes, I'm that annoying person who starts playing Christmas music in October. From the time I was a little girl, I have always loved Christmas. I mean really loved it. I've lost count of the number of Christmas sweaters, sparkly Santa hats, and light-up candy cane earrings I have. I just adore everything about the holiday—from decorating the house with lots of lights and greenery to surprising each loved one with a super special gift to reading the twelve books of Christmas to my kiddos leading up to the big day—I've always been a bit obsessive when it comes to the holiday season. (Did I mention I watch Hallmark Christmas movies year-round?)

When my father passed away and we had to endure Christmas without him, that was rough. We tried to have joy that year, but it was forced. Then, just two years later, we lost Mom and had to go through the holiday season without Mamaw or Papaw. My kids were sad. I was sad. Everything was sad.

Since then, Jeff's parents have also gone to heaven, meaning our girls have lost Mamaw and Papaw and Nana and Granddad. Though each loss impacted us differently, each one was just as painful. But you power through because that's what moms do. You put on a fake smile, don the ugly Christmas sweater, buy and wrap all the presents, decorate the tree, and bake dozens of Christmas cookies, so maybe your children won't hurt as badly as you're hurting.

At least that's what I did, but you know what? There's a better way. Whether you're experiencing loss due to a death, a divorce, a cross-country move, a family separation, or some other reason, you don't have to pretend that you're okay. It's good to be honest with yourself and your children about how you're feeling. It gives them permission to be real about their feelings too.

And you don't have to muddle through all the traditions and holiday hoopla as if it's any normal year because it's not. No matter how hard you try to make it like all of your previous holiday seasons, it won't be the same.

And that's okay.

In fact, it's a good thing.

Once I accepted that fact, I was able to let God heal my heart and infuse me with His joy, replacing the fake, manufactured kind I'd been running on for far too long. And you can do the same.

Determine today to make new memories, establish new traditions, and live in the moment. Life is too precious to waste even one day longing for what used to be and missing "the good old days." Let God put joy back into your life—not just during the holiday but every day of the year.

If you're a single mom now, sharing joint custody with your ex-husband, holidays or even weekends can be difficult because you have to share the kids. Rather than sitting at home, depressed because the kids are with their father, why not use that time to volunteer at a local soup kitchen? Or if you recently moved cross-country because of a job transfer and now you're no longer near family for holiday gatherings, why not open your home to others in your same situation? Ask your children to help you cook and decorate for that special gathering.

Get your children involved by asking them what new holiday traditions they'd like to incorporate. Get them excited about the future too! That's what we had to do. One of our new holiday traditions is shopping for the funniest gag gift (I start looking on January 1!) to put into the Family Gag Gift Exchange. Last year, Abby got stuck with these three wooden leopard snowmen I'd made (epic Pinterest fail). It was hilarious and one of our new "good old days" to remember. You know somebody is getting those leopard snowmen again this year! I can't wait.

We also started a new tradition of going cosmic bowling together after church services on New Year's Eve. And something I started a few years ago is speaking a blessing over my daughters (and now my sons-in-love) via a New Year's letter to each child. I tell them how much I love them and how special they are to me and to the kingdom of God.

No, your holidays won't be the same as they were before your loss or your move or whatever has caused you grief, but they can be just as wonderful and meaningful. Ask God to help you—He will. Your new normal, your new family traditions, your new inside jokes will become what your children call "the good old days" as they look back on their childhood with fondness.

Bethany's JETTliner

My sister is the best holiday planner ever. Her fall decorations are up earlier and earlier each year, and she makes no apologies for having her

Christmas tree set up next to her Thanksgiving table. She's amazing at creating traditions for her family. I've always envied that about her.

God really opened my eyes last year to how rotten my attitude was toward the holidays. Lugging out decorations meant more work and who was going to see them anyway? We barely have traditions of our own because we're always traveling to someone else's home for the holidays or, when we were in youth ministry and required to be at the church for holiday services, we had to rearrange schedules based on what day Christmas fell. The lack of consistency from year to year turned me into a Scrooge.

Well, no more.

Last year I decided I was going to steal a page out of my sister's book and enjoy every drop of holiday goodness with my kids. I found spike-studded pumpkins at Target and red and white Christmassy décor at Michaels.

I replaced the everyday bookshelf knickknacks with black and cream-colored pumpkins and, despite the Florida heat, embraced the change of the seasons. We watched a different Christmas movie every night. This was the first year we made and decorated Christmas cookies but it won't be the last.

I know in my heart that the likelihood of my boys living near Justin and me when they're grown is minimal. There is an adage that girls stay but boys leave, so I'm preparing my heart for that day. But here's what I forgot: that day is not this day. And if I want my boys to *want* to come home for holidays, there better be a reason—there better be some traditions and memory-making that happens *now* in order for that future to exist.

If you ever feel like you're stuck and the holidays aren't as much fun as they used to be or should be, go shopping for holiday decorations and cinnamon brooms. If your home is festive, *you'll* feel festive, and attitude is everything. And if you're not sure, follow my sister's example: set up your Christmas tree early, and let yourself enjoy the fun of the holidays.

God Calls Me Hopeful

Proverbs 4:25 says, "Let your eyes look directly forward, and your gaze be straight before you" (ESV). That doesn't mean you can't glance back and remember fondly the good times, but it does mean you can't set up camp on Memory Lane. Look forward to the future with hope! Here's my wish for you: "May the God of hope fill you with all joy and peace in believing, so that by the power of the Holy Spirit you may abound in hope" (Rom. 15:13 ESV).

Put the Merry Back into Your Christmas

If your holiday celebrations have become too commercial, or if you find yourself driving from one mandatory family gathering to the next, so worn out your kiddos don't even enjoy the season, it's time to create a new holiday tradition.

One surefire way to put the "merry" back into your holidays is to serve others. After all, it is the season of giving, is it not? Have a family meeting and discuss the best way your family can make a difference this year. Here are a few ideas to get you going:

- Set up a gift-wrapping service at your church, offering to wrap presents for anyone needing help. Accept donations for this service and give that money to a charity of your choice.

- Write Christmas cards and letters to active military servicepeople via Operation Gratitude, A Million Thanks, or the American Red Cross.

- Adopt an angel or two from your local community and buy presents for those less fortunate. (If your church doesn't have an Angel Tree, contact your local women's shelter.)
- Reach out to local nursing homes and see if your family can help with Holiday Bingo or by singing Christmas carols and distributing Christmas cards and pictures created by your budding artists.

25

They Call Me Memory Maker

Bethany's JETTliner

My mother is the Queen of Memories.

When I was old enough to drive, my sister and I received "Sister Dates" for Christmas presents. My parents gave us mall gift cards, cash for lunch, and a free Saturday with zero expectations for chores. Jill and I shopped till we dropped, then stopped at Arby's before heading home. We loved the opportunity to refresh our wardrobes for the spring semester and it gave us a chance for uninterrupted girl talk.

Similarly, my mom used her Christmas bonus money to get theme park passes. Florida residency has its perks and we spent several Sunday afternoons throughout the year at the Magic Kingdom eating hot dogs and fries from Casey's after church.

Sometimes Mom and I would go on extended grocery shopping trips, which included sneaking to an afternoon movie and splitting a popcorn and Coke.

Now that she's a grandmother (grandma codename: Malize), her memory-making genius is passed to her grandchildren. On each grand-child's tenth birthday, she celebrates their entrance to double digits with a two-day trip of their choosing.

My oldest son chose Legoland and my middle son recently celebrated with a day at ComicCon. To say my youngest is eagerly anticipating his tenth birthday is an understatement.

The example my mom set is instilled in me and my siblings. Quality time is high on all of our love language charts because our mom gave experiences merit and made the time together super special.

Here's the great news: amazing memories can be made on the cheap!

Neither Justin nor I receive Christmas bonuses anymore and with the military's fixed salary, discretionary income must be used wisely. We look for ways to create a special memory out of ordinary activities. Instead of going to the movies, we buy microwave popcorn and enjoy a night of #NetflixAndChill. Instead of eating at a restaurant for Sunday dinner, we grab Taco Bell takeout. The library is a special outing and the YMCA offers playtime for the boys (and some much-needed alone time for me).

While I've never been really good at making holiday memories, I've decided it's never too late to start. This year Justin deployed again, which meant our first Thanksgiving without him (and potentially first Christmas with him gone too). It's the weird, funny, quirky things that we remember so this year, for the first time ever, we decorated for the Christmas season on November 1. The tiny fake tree is displayed on the shelf, greenery is wrapped around our banisters, and there are plaid bows *everywhere*.

Instead of traveling on Thanksgiving, the boys and I stayed home and enjoyed a weeklong extravaganza that we now call Junk Food Jettsgiving, partially because I was sick so I Shipt-ordered a bunch of frozen snacks and meals that were easy to heat!

The Bible talks about the importance of remembering, which is why making memories is so important. First Corinthians 11:2 says "Now I commend you because you remember me in everything and maintain the traditions even as I delivered them to you" (ESV). There are countless stories in the Bible where people created memorials and I believe it's important for us to create experiences for our kids as part of that tradition.

It's funny the traditions that carry forward. The Macy's Thanksgiving Day Parade played all morning on Thanksgiving in my house as a child but not in Justin's. Yet it doesn't really feel like Thanksgiving for me unless it's playing in the background. While we may not watch the entire thing, we always stop and watch "the real Santa Claus" close out the parade at noon.

Apart from holidays, you can create memories and traditions around other types of events. College football season is a big deal in the Jett household. We host a lot of game parties and our kids get into the spirit by wearing their Florida State University (my team) or University of Miami (Justin's team) shirts or jerseys (depending on who is playing). When the two rivals play each other, the boys take sides and we enjoy great food and late nights as we stay up until the game ends.

We celebrate May the Fourth Be with You by watching a Star Wars movie on May 4, we host random dance parties throughout the day, and sometimes we grab slushies and Cow Tales candies from the gas station on hot summer days.

Our kids won't remember all the presents we bought them for their birthdays, but they'll remember that we took the time to decorate with a special themed tablecloth and streamers. They may not remember everything we do for them, but usually the small ways we make our babies feel special stay in their hearts and minds the most.

Michelle's Intel

I am all about taking pictures to capture all the wonderful memories we're making as a family, but sometimes you have to put away the camera or smartphone and just be present in the moment. And you have to be intentional about making time to make those special memories.

When was the last time you slowed down long enough to make mud pies with your kids? When was the last time you read funny poetry by a candlelight pizza dinner? If it's been a while, then plan a special day to do nothing but fun stuff with your children. Of course, this works much better if your kids are willing to spend an entire day with you. Once they reach puberty, our teens have their own little social worlds and packed schedules, but if you still have little ones or tweens running around, why not host an all-out fun-filled day?

Watch funny, family films in your jammies until noon. Then, if the weather is nice, take a bike ride together, or go on a scavenger hunt in a nearby park. Play board games until nightfall. Finish the day with devotions and prayer time. Just bask in one another's presence, soaking it all in.

There's nothing quite like a full day with the people you love most in this world.

Even now, though my girls are grown and married, we still plan special family times. We just have to plan a little further out in order to ensure both girls and their spouses can join us. Last year, we all met up for a Cubs versus Reds game (thankfully, my girls chose mates who are also Chicago Cubs fans, so we lucked out!) followed by dinner and a hotel stay in downtown Cincy. The next morning, we walked down the street and shared a late breakfast before everyone went their separate ways. I loved that weekend so much!

Other times, the kids will all come to our house and we'll host a euchre (Midwest card game) tournament. I'll order their favorite pizza, and we'll finish the night watching one of our go-to funny movies. I cherish those times.

Make memories with your children when they're young, and when they're older, they'll long for those times and keep coming back for more.

God Calls Me to Keep His Traditions

Scripture tells us to keep the traditions as long as they don't interfere with the teaching of Christ: "Stand firm and hold to the traditions that you were taught by us, either by our spoken word or by our letter" (2 Thess. 2:15 ESV). Human traditions are important but only as long as we don't "break the command of God for the sake of your tradition" (Matt. 15:3). Let's impress God's commands on our children's hearts so that Scripture will infiltrate their memories.

Five Love Languages

The Five Love Languages is an amazing book by Dr. Gary Chapman that changed everything about how Justin and I communicated when we were dating, how we interact with others, and how we raise our kids. It's a must-read for anyone who wants to love others better, and it provides a deeper insight into why we do the things that *we* do. You can take a free quiz to discover your love language at 5lovelanguages.com.

26

They Call Me Best Present Giver Ever (at Least One of Them Does)

Michelle's Intel

When I took Gary Chapman's *The Five Love Languages* test, I discovered my top love language is gifts, followed closely by words of affirmation. Basically, if you buy me a present and brag on me a bit, I'm one happy mama. If you haven't taken the love language test, I suggest you do. It's amazing how much you can learn about yourself and how much you can help others in your life understand you. And, while you're at it, have your children also take the test so you'll know their individual love languages and be better able to address their needs.

I wish I'd taken the test long before I actually did, and I wish I'd had my children take the test, too, because I think it could've prevented some family heartache along the way.

I'll never forget coming home from a business trip with gifts in hand for both of my girls. I'd stumbled onto an amazing little boutique in my travels and purchased jewelry I was sure both girls would absolutely adore. Ally excitedly searched through the tissue paper, found her earrings and necklace set, and immediately put them on. She hugged me and thanked me. She was thrilled! Ab, on the other hand, mumbled, "Thanks, Mom" as she retreated to the couch to finish her homework. She didn't open her present right away, and when she did, I found the earrings and bracelet I'd purchased for her lying on her desk.

It hurt my feelings that Abby didn't seem to appreciate the gifts I had chosen especially for her. We never talked about it, and eventually, I noticed Ally wearing the jewelry I had purchased for Abby. When I asked her, Ally simply said, "She didn't want it, so I decided to try it on. I like it."

This type of scenario played out many times over the years, yet I never could figure out why Abby reacted the way she did. In fact, I finally quit buying her anything if she wasn't with me because I knew I wouldn't be able to please her. I thought she didn't like what I bought her because I tend to like more blingy things than she does. Sometimes I thought she just didn't like me. But neither of those things were true.

It wasn't until this past year that I finally understood. Abby and her husband, Micah, needed a babysitter for their baby, my first grandson, Bear. Their regular nanny was ill, and they didn't have any backups. I was just in from speaking at a women's ministry event so I was already packed. I simply kissed my hubby goodbye, loaded up the jeep, and headed for their house three hours away. I was happy to help; plus, I'm always looking for an excuse to spend more time with Baby Bear. That week was a blur, but it was a blissful blur. Bear and I had a blast together during the day, and when Abby arrived home after teaching each day, we ordered dinner in, played with Bear, and watched Netflix after putting the baby to bed. It was relaxing and wonderful.

On Friday, as I was getting ready to leave, Abby hugged me and said,

"Thanks so much for coming down and helping out, Mom. I love having you here. I wish you could stay forever."

That's when it hit me . . . her love language is quality time.

You see, I'd been praying for a breakthrough with Abby. I wanted to be closer; I just didn't know how to accomplish it.

Message received, Lord, I thought.

When I want to bless Abby, I'll surprise her by stopping by for lunch on my way to a speaking engagement. And when I want to make Ally smile, I'll ship her our favorite Bath & Body Works scented candle in the white-and-gray-marble packaging.

Different girls, different love languages, same blessed mama.

Yes, I wish I'd discovered Abby's love language years ago so I might've been more of what she needed, but you know what? It's never too late.

It's never too late to show love in a greater way. It's never too late to be a better parent. It's never too late to let the love of God fill you up so that you're overflowing in His unconditional love. It's never too late to be used by Him.

So go forth, Mama, and love bigger, better, and greater.

Your love will be right on time.

Bethany's JETTliner

The love languages are a big part of Jett-household communication, so while our boys are little, we strive to nurture each of the five different types: words of affirmation, quality time, acts of service, physical touch, and receiving gifts. Not only do we respond positively to our highest love language, but we also lash out with our love language when we're angry.

This information means that we can nurture our kids' hearts and, on the opposite side, make punishments more effective.

My middle son's love language is touch. He's always been a cuddle-bug, even from the first few minutes of his life. He's the best snuggler. Conversely, he's the first of our children to hit or punch, which drives me absolutely crazy.

My older son was more difficult to figure out, but we finally realized his love language is quality time. Parenting became more intentional and I made sure to include him in situations I didn't think of before, like sitting at the table with me instead of being on the couch or chair, or inviting him to go with me to check the mail. This also helped with punishments because being grounded is more effective for him than anything else.

We're still figuring out my youngest son's love language, but I'm pretty sure that words of affirmation and physical touch are high on his list.

The Bible says to train each child in the way he should go, and I believe it means to raise each child specifically for that child's individual needs. Knowing our kids' love languages and intentionally parenting them in the way they need to be parented and loved makes for well-adjusted and happy kids.

God Calls Me to Love Better

First John 3:18 says, "Dear children, let's not merely say that we love each other; let us show the truth by our actions" (NLT). I'm sure you've heard the expression, "Actions speak louder than words." So put your love in action today where your family is concerned. Love your children the way they need to be loved.

Simple Ways to Love Your Children Better

Even though your kiddos probably have different love languages, here are five ways to show love to your littles and not-so-littles.

- Spend one-on-one time with each child: Schedule Mommy-child dates where you let your little one pick the activity. Make a big deal out of it with a special invitation and build up to the big day!

- Put love notes inside your child's lunch box or love sticky notes on the rearview mirror in your teen's car.

- Give your child the best gift of all—your undivided attention.

- Do proximity hugs—any time your child walks by you, pull that kiddo in for a quick hug. (Your tweens and teens may not "love" this as much as you do.)

- Brag on your child for a job well done whenever that happens to be the case.

27

I Call Myself Failure

Bethany's JETTliner

I collapsed into myself like a dying star after my oldest child was born. I'd quit my full-time job to move to Tampa when I was eight months pregnant and my husband's job as a youth minister was in limbo because our church and another church merged. Which youth minister was going to be let go?

We were scraping by on one income, living in an apartment that cost half of his monthly paycheck, my family was two hours away, and I had no friends in the area.

It was a recipe for disaster.

It was a recipe for postpartum depression.

Postpartum depression is hard to talk about.

It's even harder to write about because the words are in black and white.

What I thought were the "baby blues" ended up being an eighteen-month ordeal. I couldn't handle my emotions, I felt distant from my newborn, I had zero energy to do anything, I felt like a stranger in my body, and those baby blues turned into a darkness that I've blocked out of my mind.

When our expenses exceeded our income, we turned to credit cards, and when the credit card statements came, I left them unopened and unpaid.

I was failing as a wife and a mother and scared to death to open my mouth about what I was feeling. I found myself afraid to be alone with my son. What if I lost my mind and turned into one of those psycho-crazy killers you see in movies? What if I did something that I'd regret?

Would they take my baby away?

Would they put me on medication that would dull my senses even more than they were?

Would my husband wish he'd never married me?

What was I doing?

Was I losing my mind?

How could I believe in God and feel this way?

Would it be easier on my family if I weren't part of the equation anymore?

Every morning that I could, I packed up the baby and rode with Justin to the church so I wouldn't be alone.

Anytime I felt brave enough to mention to a friend a hint of what was happening, the response was the same. "All moms go through this. It will end soon."

But it never did.

The internet became my lifeline. I pored over the articles that outlined postpartum depression. I found myself agreeing with the symptoms and diagnosis from the blog posts but it was a hard label to self-assess.

One site promised help. There was a contact link where you could email a counselor. It was safer than talking in person, so I reached out.

And a counselor reached back.

She was local to the area and gently suggested I come to her office, but I didn't want a paper trail or a permanent diagnosis.

It wasn't until Jeremy was eighteen months old that I finally gave in. Justin and I went together. She asked questions and in between massive sobs I shared what was happening. About halfway into the session, she took a piece of paper from her desk and handed it to me.

"These are nine stressors that can lead up to or cause postpartum depression. You have eight."

"So I really do have postpartum depression?"

"Yes."

And the heaviness left my shoulders as the weight of wondering was released.

The counselor shared coping techniques and communication strategies that Justin and I could work through, and recommended follow-up appointments.

There was hope.

One of the methods that Justin and I implemented right away was complete honesty about how I felt. If a wave of darkness or depression washed over me, I immediately shared that with him. He took over whatever I was doing, and I was free to go into our room and be alone for fifteen minutes, giving myself time to feel better. Then fifteen minutes became ten. Then it became five.

If you feel like you can't cope or are struggling with depression or baby blues, you are not alone. You are not crazy. I wish I'd talked to a doctor or counselor *much* earlier than I did. I shouldn't have waited so long. There are coping skills, support groups, and medications that help. Whichever path you choose is your decision, but I urge you to take the first step and talk about it. Don't let Satan bully you into keeping it a secret or making you feel worthless.

David wrote psalm after psalm expressing his depression and anguish. The man after God's own heart showed us the perfect example of a healthy way to deal with those emotions. Share. Talk. Vent. Write. Pray.

I was nervous that the postpartum depression would rear its ugly head with my second baby. There were a few times I felt overwhelmed, and again, I'd excuse myself for a few minutes until the anxiety eased. With my third child, I barely experienced it at all.

Please talk to someone, and if you know someone who has had a baby, please check in on her. She may be feeling overwhelmed and worthless on the inside, and knowing you will love her no matter what can mean everything to her.

Michelle's Intel

Though I've never struggled with postpartum depression, I know what it's like to feel desperate. And I know what it's like to be mad at God.

I had been praying and believing for my mama to be completely healed and restored to perfect health, but the cancer seemed to be winning the battle. Our whole family stood in faith for Mom's healing, yet she had taken a turn for the worse and her diagnosis was grim.

Mom and I had been watching lots of *Murder, She Wrote* reruns over the past few weeks as I sat next to her hospital bed, but today I needed more than Angela Lansbury could offer. I needed to hear from God. As I flipped through the channels, I finally stopped on a Joyce Meyer broadcast. Mom and I both liked her ministry. She always encouraged me, but on this particular day, she had a direct message from the Master for me.

I tried to listen but I was so restless . . . and mad. Yes, I was mad at God. I couldn't understand why He hadn't healed my mom. I'd known of so many others He had supernaturally healed. In fact, I'd written about several!

My thoughts were interrupted by Joyce's voice, saying, "You can't get mad at God . . . because He is the only one who can get you through this."[7]

It's like she was talking directly to me.

Tears streamed down my face. I knew God was telling me that although I would never understand, I would have to trust Him anyway, and He would love me through it.

Mama let go of my hand and took the Savior's hand a few days later.

I was devastated, yes, but for the first time in a long time, I wasn't mad at God. And I could receive His love once again.

If you're in a desperate place, don't stay mad at God; run to Him! He loves you, and He wants to love you through whatever you're facing today.

You can trust Him; I speak from experience.

God Calls Me to Not Fear

When our thoughts are dark and our hearts are heavy, we must trust that God is with us . . . even if we can't feel His presence. When I'm struggling, I cling to Psalm 23:4: "Though I walk through the valley of the shadow of death, I will fear no evil; for You are with me" (NKJV). Depression is a valley, but God is with you and you can reach the other side.

Depression Resources

Here are a few resources in case you or someone you know is suffering from any form of depression or postpartum depression in particular:

- Postpartum Support International: http://www.postpartum.net or 1-800-944-4773.

---

7. Joyce Meyer, from a televised sermon Michelle viewed on May 3, 2006.

- Find local support groups: http://www.postpartum.net/get-help/locations/.
- The American College of Obstetricians and Gynecologists resource: https://www.acog.org/Womens-Health/Depression-and-Postpartum-Depression.
- Inkblot Therapy is an online video counseling service (currently in Canada only): https://ink.inkblottherapy.com.
- National Institute of Mental Health resources and symptoms list: https://www.nimh.nih.gov/health/publications/postpartum-depression-facts/index.shtml.

28

They Call Me Mama Bear

Michelle's Intel

We moved from Fort Worth, Texas, back to our hometown in southern Indiana in 2006 because my precious mama was battling cancer, and we wanted to spend every last minute with her we could. While the girls loved their mamaw very much, they were not happy about leaving all their friends behind in Fort Worth.

Texas was really the only home they'd ever known, since we'd moved to Fort Worth when Abby was five and Ally was three. And now, with Ally starting sixth grade and Abby starting seventh, we had taken them away from life as they'd always known it.

It was not a happy time in our household.

But we tried to make the best of it. We went new school clothes shopping. I took them to my old middle school and showed them around. We prayed they would have favor with their teachers and fellow students, and when their first day at their new school arrived, they were ready. So, you can imagine my surprise when I received a call from the secretary that first week of school, asking me to stop by the office for a visit with the principal.

"What's this regarding?" I asked, thinking I needed to sign more transfer paperwork.

"It's about Abby."

"What's wrong—is she sick?"

"No, it's not that . . . I think you should hear it from the parties involved," she said.

"I'll be right there," I answered and headed to the school.

Once inside, I saw Abby sitting right outside the inner office. She was bawling.

"I didn't do anything, Mommy," she cried. "I promise. I don't even know why I'm in trouble."

I believed her.

"It'll be okay, Ab," I said. "I'll be right back."

I walked into the inner office and greeted the principal—a man I really liked and respected—and a teacher I'd never met. Over the next few minutes, this teacher accused Abby of talking back and being disrespectful. Now, here's the thing. I knew my oldest could have a mouth on her from time to time, but usually only to me. Every single teacher she'd had at Eagle Mountain Elementary in Texas raved about Abby's sweet heart and work ethic. I just wasn't buying it.

"That's very surprising," I calmly said. "What exactly did she say?"

After the teacher explained what Abby had said to land her in the principal's office, I shook my head in disbelief. Abby was in trouble for answering, "Yes, ma'am." This teacher thought Ab was being sassy and sarcastic by answering, "Yes, ma'am," but Abby always answered that way because it's the Texas way. If you didn't answer "Yes, ma'am" at her previous school, you would've been in trouble for being disrespectful. I explained that very point.

I could tell this teacher wasn't hearing me, or at least she wasn't believing me. So, I went on to share a lesson in Manners 101 and pointed out that she could probably benefit from such a lesson. Furthermore, I let her know I didn't appreciate her making Abby's first week at the new school so difficult.

I could feel the Mama Bear in me coming out; there was no turning back. I was on a mission to defend and protect my child. I wasn't ugly, but I was firm. Lastly, I asked this teacher to apologize to Abby for misjudging and embarrassing her. I thanked the nice principal for his time, locked eyes with the teacher one more time so she knew I meant business, and I left with Abby. We drove directly to Jiffy Treat for some Superman ice cream, which always made everything better.

Even now as I share this story with you, my heart is racing and my inner Mama Bear is restless. The Mama Bear instinct is strong in us, isn't it? Our need to protect our young is so strong, in fact, at times it simply takes over. I'll never apologize for defending my children in the face of injustice, but conversely, I've always been the first one to discipline my little darlings when they have acted ugly. There has to be a balance.

I think it's important for our kids to know we have their backs and that we'll fight for them in the midst of unfair or hostile circumstances. But I also think it's equally important they know we'll be the first to punish them if they are disrespectful or bratty.

You know, our heavenly Father made us innately protective because it's a good thing. After all, He has that same nature. He is quite protective where His children are concerned. He says in His Word that no weapon formed against us shall prosper and every tongue that rises against us shall be stilled (Isa. 54:17). His Word also says, "God is our refuge and strength, always ready to help in times of trouble" (Ps. 46:1 NLT).

I say if you have a Mama Bear shirt, wear it with pride!

Bethany's JETTliner

My first experience with the fire-in-the-belly Mama Bear feeling happened at church.

On a Sunday morning.

And was directed at a two-year-old.

Talk about feeling like a monster.

I'd volunteered to help in the nursery, mostly because I now had a child who needed to be *in* the nursery.

I sat in the rocking chair and listened to the sermon playing through the TV speakers in the room while the little ones played.

My fourteen-month-old clutched a ball and jumped up and down.

Then it happened.

A bigger child marched up to my sweet little firstborn and pushed him down.

Even still, in my mind's eye I see the scenario through a camera lens, like an out-of-body experience. My baby got knocked to the ground, the ball flew out of his hands, and my focus zoomed in on this little monster child who dared hurt my son.

My entire body felt hot inside. I swooped in and scooped up my baby, all the while fighting back this ridiculous but very real desire to retaliate. Against a two-year-old.

For someone who didn't feel like she had the maternal gene growing up, I realized that some instincts reveal themselves at the opportune time. And although I felt like a psycho for my reactionary feelings, I cuddled my baby, told the two-year-old to be kind, and rocked for all of the fifteen seconds my energetic son would let me hold him until he was ready to chase the ball again.

I also realized that a mother's love is fierce and for the first time I understood how God must feel when we, His children, get hurt. And even though I determined that nursery duty was probably not my forte, I felt closer to my heavenly Father for the experience of earning my Mama Bear badge.

God Calls Me Protected

If there's anyone who will understand your Mama Bear instincts, it's our heavenly Father. Psalm 91:1–2 says, "Those who live in the shelter of the Most High will find rest in the shadow of the Almighty. This I declare about the LORD: He alone is my refuge, my place of safety; he is my God, and I trust him" (NLT). You can trust God. He's got your back.

When to Growl and When to Grin and Bear It

Here's the thing. To be a good Mama Bear, you can't fight your child's battles all the time. Good Mama Bears only intervene when the child can't fight alone. For example, if your child is being bullied in the school cafeteria and you've already alerted the powers that be, yet the bullying continues, it's time for Mama Bear to come out and play. But if your child is constantly bickering with another girl at dance class, let the kiddos work it out. Mama Bear doesn't need to get involved.

Knowing when to intervene and when to let your child handle the situation will determine whether you're a good Mama Bear or a bad Mama Bear. If you're always there to fight your children's battles, then your little cubs will never develop the skills needed to defend themselves. Don't be afraid to let your little cubs be their own advocates; however, like any good Mama Bear, watch from a distance and be ready to protect and defend as needed.

29

They Call Me Ma'am

Bethany's JETTliner

Do you remember the first time someone called you *ma'am*?
I was in a drive-through line when it happened to me. The teenager handed me my soda and said, "Here you go, ma'am."

I was twenty-three.

I hated it.

Thus, I swore I would never make my children call me *ma'am*. I thought it sounded too formal, and I wanted to have a friendly and close relationship with my children. *Ma'am* and *sir* weren't required in my house as a child and I turned out just fine.

Then I had all boys.

Boys that would grow up to be bigger than me.

Boys that needed to learn from a young age to respect their mama.

And even though not everyone considers Florida to be part of "the South," we have enough of a cultural bubble trickling down that makes *ma'am* and *sir* entirely appropriate.

We've chosen to have our kids say *yes* instead of *yeah* and *ma'am* or *sir* when they are being disciplined or called.

My youngest is the best at this. "Yes, ma'am" flows out of his mouth like honey, and the repetition of using it at home with me transfers to other adults.

How do you teach your kids to use certain words?

We practice.

While running errands, the car is the perfect teaching place because your kids are basically forced to listen to whatever you say. I call out a phrase and the boys repeat it, usually in a singsong way. Instead of muscle memory, we practice mental memory.

"Yes, please." *"Yes, please."*

"No, thank you." *"No, thank you."*

"Yes, ma'am. No, ma'am." *"Yes, ma'am. No, ma'am."*

"Yes, sir. No, sir." *"Yes, sir. No, sir."*

We also want our kids to respond a certain way when they are called. When I was growing up, my dad expected my siblings and me to appear when he called our name. Yelling back "Whaaaaat?" was not allowed.

If I say my son's name, he'll typically respond with "Ma'am?" or "Yes, Mommy?" which is exactly what I'm hoping for. Those two simple phrases are respectful and indicate he is listening.

When it becomes second nature at home, I know it will be second nature when he's somewhere without me. My husband's military influence also plays a part in our decision to say *ma'am* and *sir*, but even if these aren't terms you use in your home, the idea of teaching children to respect adults and those in authority is the same. This concept teaches kids to humble themselves and honor the other person.

However, the opposite is also true. Just because my kids say *ma'am* or *sir* doesn't mean they are being respectful. If their tone is sarcastic or gruff then respect is lost from the words.

The attitude is really and truly the heart of the matter.

Sometimes *ma'am* and *sir* aren't appropriate. The adults who work in the Sunday school areas and nurseries don't necessarily want to be called *ma'am* or *sir*, so often they are referred to with Ms. or Mr. preceding their first name.

Ms. Bethany.

Mr. Justin.

Ms. Michelle.

My children play online games with our good friends in Michigan. Sometimes Justin and our friend Cyle will play with the kids and I'll hear my boys yell, "Ugh, Cy-le!"

I'm quick to respond, "Mr. Cyle," which they repeat, because even when adults are playing a game they don't lose the respect that they are owed.

I understand this is often a regional thing, since in some areas of the United States it is proper manners to say Mrs. Last Name and Mr. Last Name. The point is to help our kids do what is respectful no matter where they find themselves.

Now that doesn't always mean straitlaced Goody Two-shoes all the time. Sometimes we need to make space for personalities and fun. So even though my kids use *ma'am* to refer to me at different times, I'm also at various times lovingly called Mommy-Mo-Mo (thanks, Phineas and Ferb) and Eda-maw-may (from Disney's *Bedtime for Garbanzo* YouTube videos).

The beautiful thing about being a mom is that you get to choose the terminology you want for your household. Exodus 20:12 says for children to honor their parents. By teaching our kids to respect their elders, we are also teaching them to respect God.

So do your thing, girlfriend. It's never too late to instill respect . . . even on days when you're Mommy-Mo-Mo.

Michelle's Intel

Yep, I remember the first time I was called *ma'am*. Ironically, it was also at a drive-through. I was twenty-eight, and we had just moved to Texas. Like my coauthor, I also hated it. The term *ma'am* made me feel so old. But I soon discovered it wasn't that my antiaging face cream wasn't working; *ma'am* was simply a respectful way of addressing me, and that fine young man at the Dairy Queen drive-through had been raised right.

Both of my girls picked up on the "yes, ma'am," "no, sir" thing very quickly because their school required it, and it has served them well in life for the most part (see the Mama Bear devo).

It's funny how a title can make you feel differently. As moms, we wear many hats and answer to many names—some we love; some not so much—but we still answer. Because every single name we bear is a part of our "mom makeup." Names have a way of defining us. God has many names, each one describing who He is—Abba means "Daddy, Father," El Elyon means "God Most High," and El Shaddai means "God Almighty," just to name a few.

Yes, I'm a wifey. I'm a mom. I'm a ma'am. And, last year, I became a grandmother, but if you ever call me Granny or Mamaw or Grandma or Nana, we will no longer be friends, lol.

Seriously, though, when I found out Abby was pregnant with our first grandchild, I immediately knew what names I didn't want, but I had a hard time settling on one I liked. My sister had already claimed "Mimi" so I tried on "Gigi" for size, and I liked it. Of course, my grandson isn't talking yet, so I have no idea what he will actually end up calling me, but whatever it is, I'm sure I'll love it because I adore him.

It's important we teach our children to honor their elders, and it's important we embrace all our titles, even the ones that make us feel old. We can rock each and every one!

God Calls Me to Teach My Children to Love Him

Perhaps the biggest responsibility we have as mothers is to teach our precious babies to love our God and follow Jesus. In Proverbs we are told to not forsake our mother's teaching (Prov. 1:8) and that a child who is left to himself brings shame to his mother (Prov. 29:15). There are many decisions our children will make on their own, and choosing to follow Jesus is one of them, but we cannot be lackadaisical in our approach. The world is ready to chew up our kids and spit them out so by teaching our children to respect the Word of God, to love Him above all else, to respect our neighbors and take care of those who need help, we instill a servant's heart and honor God by doing so. When we live out our faith boldly, we encourage our children to follow this example so that one day they can teach their own children how to follow the Lord.

How to Model Respect

Our children soak up information like sponges. You can teach your kids respect by correcting their behavior when they are disrespectful, but also by modeling it.

- If you do something that offends your children, apologize. We all make mistakes and our kids need to see what a respectful apology looks like.

- Show respect to waitstaff or people in service industries by talking calmly and rationally when something goes wrong.

- If someone is rude or disrespectful, point it out to your kids and have them share how the situation could have been handled differently.

- Show respect to your spouse and friends and acknowledge the times when you don't.

- Respect the boundaries you set for your children. If the rule in your home is that kids need to knock, model that by knocking on their bedroom doors. (In our house, the kids' doors are never allowed to be shut, but we still knock as a courtesy.)

- Guard your boundaries. At a certain age, children should respect Mommy's bathroom time, so barring an emergency, the kids must wait.

30

They Call Me Scaredy-Cat

Michelle's Intel

Growing up, I was never a scaredy-cat. No, I was always more of a risk taker—someone who wasn't afraid to go for "it" whatever "it" happened to be. And, during the times when my confidence started to waver due to obstacles in my path or an all-out attack from an adversary, my parents were there to encourage me, pray over me, and send me back out into the world with renewed courage.

But all that changed when I became a parent. Suddenly, "scaredy-cat" became my middle name. Sure, I'd researched the whole parenthood thing prior to giving birth to our first daughter, but when I officially became a mom that snowy December afternoon, I was not prepared for the onslaught of emotions. Of course, I was filled with joy and awe and thankfulness for this adorable little baby girl staring up at me. But I was also filled with insecurity, doubt, and full-on fear. I remember holding Abby, who was only minutes old at the time, and thinking, "I can't believe they are going to let us take you home . . . we have no idea what we're doing."

That first week home was rough. Abby was not taking to nursing like I'd hoped, so she was hungry all the time, which meant she cried all the time. I was so stressed over the situation, I was afraid my milk might dry up. But I was even more afraid that my baby girl might become malnourished simply because I couldn't figure out how to nurse her properly.

On that fifth night home from the hospital, I was up doing a late-night feeding so I turned on the TV and switched from Country Music Television to QVC, thinking I might do a little Christmas shopping. After all, I was an accomplished multitasker.

But Abby wasn't cooperating. She wouldn't latch on. I'd met with the lactation coach at the hospital and learned the all-important "football hold" but still, Abby struggled to eat. I was tired. My nipples were bleeding. And Abby was screaming because she was hungry. I was determined not to supplement with formula after my meeting with the lactation coach who encouraged me to "stick with it," promising it would get easier.

I wasn't so sure.

Just when I thought I'd finally calmed Abby enough to try latching on again, she projectile vomited blood—everywhere. The wall behind our rocker looked like a scene straight out of a horror flick.

I frantically dialed the twenty-four-hour number for our pediatrician and barely said hello before shouting into the phone that my baby had just vomited blood—everywhere. I was being transferred to an on-call nurse when Jeff stumbled into the living room, took one look at the bloody wall, and said, "Dear Lord! What happened in here?"

I wanted to answer but I was crying louder and harder than Abby—I was so scared. *What if she has some rare disease that prevents her from eating? What if she ingested something sharp? What if she's allergic to my milk? What if . . .*

Just then, a very calming voice came through the phone and said, "Everything is going to be all right."

I recognized that voice. It was the nurse who'd been with me in the delivery room just a few days earlier.

"Are your nipples irritated?" she asked. (There's a question no one had ever asked me before, lol.)

"Yes, they're both bleeding," I answered. "I'm a mess."

"Well, that's probably why your baby vomited blood. It's nothing to be too concerned about, although you should probably call your pediatrician back during office hours and let him know what's going on. Why don't you give your breasts a rest and supplement with formula for a few feedings and see how that goes . . . And, hey, don't worry. You're doing great!"

Fear that had blanketed my heart and our home for the past week lifted all at once. I knew I had much to learn about being a mom, but I also realized I didn't have to be an instant expert, nor did I have to be afraid. God had called me to be a mom, so He would equip me to be Mom. Meanwhile, He had given me an awesome support system—from my supportive hubby to my parents who had moved next door to my extended family to the sweet nurse who took the time to reassure me that everything was going to be all right.

After Jeff went back to bed, I turned off QVC and tuned in to God. It was really the first time I'd been calm since coming home from the hospital. Abby must've also sensed the peace because she snuggled into me as I gave her a bottle. As I listened to her sweet baby gulps (she was hungry), I prayed that God would help me be the mom she needed me to be, not just that night but her whole life through. And I prayed He would help me stop worrying over every little thing and instead press into Him the way Abby was pressing into me—with total trust, peace, and contentment.

That's still the prayer of my heart. I hope you'll make it the prayer of yours too. And, hey, don't worry . . . you're doing a great job.

Bethany's JETTliner

Being overly anxious or paranoid is not a positive trait, so I'm not sure it was a great idea for me to minor in criminal justice. After taking classes on serial killers and sex crimes, I have an internal voice that never stops, especially when I've got my kids with me in public.

I've had to learn to manage my reactions and emotions so that I didn't pass on negative traits to my boys. A healthy awareness is one thing; an unhealthy mistrust of everyone and everything is quite another. Not only do I not want to raise paranoid children, but I also need my boys to see me as their safe place. They need to trust and not be afraid, so I have to trust and not be afraid as well.

I have moments where I'm a scaredy-cat for real, like just last night I had to pick up our son from a youth event. I was the first parent to arrive at the house, which was toward the back of the property with zero lights.

I made Justin stay on the phone with me until the others showed up.

Beyond those moments, we must realize and teach our kids that God is our eternal safe place and He is always here to calm our spirits and grant us protection.

God Calls Me Brave

First Corinthians 16:13 says, "Keep alert. Be firm in your faith. Stay brave and strong" (CEV). Well, to "stay" brave and strong, that means I must already be those things, right? And so are you! Let's stay brave and strong and be godly examples for our children as we take this faith walk together.

Don't Go It Alone—Ask for Help

Coming home from the hospital with a new baby can be a bit overwhelming, whether you've chosen to bottle-feed, breastfeed, or some combination of the two. Your instinct to nest can still be in overdrive during this season, and yet you're probably too tired to put away all the baby gifts you received from hospital well-wishers; do all the laundry that must be done; or deep clean the car seat your infant just hurled all over during your trip home from the hospital.

And that's okay.

Rest.

One of the best pieces of advice I ever received from my lactation consultant was simply, "Let others do the cooking, cleaning, and organizing while you focus on feeding your baby. No one else can breastfeed but you."

Little did she know, but that advice gave me permission to rest, feed my baby girl, pump when needed, and ask for help with everything else. Up to that point, I'd never been too big on asking for help. I don't know if it was a pride thing or a control thing, but I had a very hard time receiving assistance from anyone—even when others offered. But, after the lactation consultant offered those words of wisdom, asking for help wasn't as difficult. In fact, it felt good. So, don't try to be a superhero. Ask for help. Let your church or moms group do a meal rotation for you. Let your mother-in-law go grocery shopping for you. Let your spouse change the majority of dirty diapers. And let yourself ease into this amazing season of your life.

31

They Call Me Bad Dreams Destroyer

Bethany's JETTliner

Professional dream analysts believe that our dreams are a continuation of the day's thought processes.[8] Anxiety is a common nightmare trigger, and never have my boys suffered more bad dreams than when my husband was deployed overseas.

It's one thing to scare away the bogeyman and check closets for ghosts, but it was a different ball game when the monsters in the dreams were beheading their daddy night after night.

How do you comfort a child who is dreaming of death?

How do you chase away their nightmare when it's yours as well?

When I had a nightmare as a little girl, I'd clutch my teddy bear

---

8. Lizette Borreli, "A Bad Dream Is More Than Just a Dream: The Science of Nightmares," Medical Daily, March 31, 2015, https://www.medicaldaily.com/bad-dream-more-just -dream-science-nightmares-327586.

Kirby, slip my legs over the side of the bed, and creep into the hallway. Then I'd tiptoe into my parents' room, which was barely lit by the moonlight sneaking through the curtains, just enough light to maneuver baskets of laundry and kicked-off shoes.

When I reached my daddy's side of the bed, I'd touch his shoulder softly so he'd wake without being startled. "I had a bad dream," were the only words needed. He'd give me a hug, pat my shoulder, and pray for God to remove all the scary feelings and the bad dreams, keep me safe, and let me fall asleep quickly with sweet dreams.

With the bad dreams taken care of, I'd pad my way back to my room, feeling along the hallway wall for my door, and slide back into my sheets with the Rainbow Brite covers. I'd repeat my daddy's prayer over and over in my mind until I fell asleep.

Nightmares can be frightening, but sharing the dream out loud can help eliminate some of the fear.

Even as a teenager, if a dream was bad enough, I'd still wake up my daddy so he'd say a prayer over me before I went back to sleep. And as a mother to my three boys, being awakened for nightmare prayers is a role I happily accept.

The Bible says that if you lie down, you will not be afraid; when you lie down, your sleep will be sweet (Prov. 3:24). Scripture also says to resist the devil and he will flee from you (James 4:7). This is a verse I'd repeat continuously, and for good measure, I would often grab my Bible and slide it under my pillow. The feel of the leather cover and the comfort of the words helped calm my mind and spirit.

Another comforting verse is from Psalm 23:4: "Even though I walk through the darkest valley, I will not be afraid, for you are close beside me. Your rod and your staff protect and comfort me" (NLT).

I clung to these verses when it was my turn to be the nightmare comforter, the Bad Dreams Destroyer. My boys are not as quiet as I was as a child. I'm often awakened by them barreling into my room or by their cries of terror when the dreams are too paralyzing for them to get to me. They touch my arm, tell me they had a bad dream, and drop their head onto my shoulder as I wrap my arms around them and kiss their foreheads. I hold them for a few minutes, letting the weight of my hug reassure them. Then I whisper a prayer into their ears, asking God to protect them, to wipe away all memories of the nightmare, to let them sleep peacefully and calmly the rest of the night.

When they're ready, they give me a final squeeze and head back to their beds, although when they were younger, I'd either scoop them into my arms and cuddle them to sleep or tuck them back into their beds and rub their backs until they fell asleep.

Never underestimate the power of prayer over our children. We may not be able to control the dreams our children have but we believe in the God who is the ultimate Bad Dreams Destroyer. He promises to give us peace and we can pray that peace over our precious littles as they sleep.

Michelle's Intel

My girls were very young when our country was attacked on 9/11. Though we tried to limit the amount of news coverage they saw about the Twin Towers coming down and the planes crashing, we couldn't shield them from all of it. Unfortunately, as a writer and an inspirational speaker, I am flying somewhere at least once a month.

Several nights after 9/11, I was putting the girls to bed, reminding them that I would be flying out the following day because I had to speak at a women's conference, and they became hysterical. I tried to calm them down, but nothing worked. Just when I was about to call for Jeffrey, the Holy Spirit dropped this verse into my heart: "For God has not given us a spirit of fear, but of power and of love and of a sound mind" (2 Tim. 1:7 NKJV).

I quoted the verse out loud for them, and then I said: "Say this with me, girls: I will not be afraid at all!"

They shouted back, "I will not be afraid at all!"

We did this several more times, getting louder every time.

And so began our new nighttime ritual. It worked when they were afraid of storms, monsters in the closet, spiders, bees, or when I had to get on an airplane.

Out of this nighttime ritual was birthed my children's picture book, *I Will Not Be Afraid*. That book has been calming children's fears for more than a decade, proof that God can take what the devil meant for your harm (or your children's harm) and turn it into good (Gen. 50:20).

God Calls Me to Be at Peace

Our minds are powerful and our dreams can be so vividly real that it's hard to fall asleep. Psalm 46:1 says that God is our refuge, an ever-present help in trouble, and when we're dealing with intangible forces like dreams, only God can help. When we pray at bedtime we ask for legions of angels to be around us and for God to give us a hedge of protection while we sleep. I petition God for sweet dreams for my boys and to keep the Evil One far away from us.

The Bible tells us not to be worried or anxious about anything but to make our requests known to God so that His peace, which surpasses all understanding, will be given to us (Phil. 4:6–7). What an incredible comfort when we're scared or terrified. Speak these verses over your children, during the times when you're scared, or when bad dreams rear their ugly heads. Repeat these verses to yourself and know that God has you, loves you, and can chase those bad dreams away.

Ways to Fall Asleep Peacefully

- Dim the lights so your internal clock kicks in that it's bedtime.

- Stop looking at screens of any kind a few hours before bed.

- Read a book.

- Play soothing music.

- Drink a warm glass of milk (some people swear by this).

- If your doctor allows, try a sleep aid or sleepy-time tea.

- Lower the temperature on the thermostat.

32

They Call Me Spunky

Michelle's Intel

As we tried to fit in with our new Texas hometown, it seemed only appropriate to take the fam to a Friday night rodeo in Cowtown. We sat very close to the action, close enough to have dirt occasionally flung in our direction. It was all very exciting! And then the announcer called for all the children under the age of twelve to come down and join him in the center of the arena. My youngest daughter, Allyson, who was only four at the time, ran past me, shot down the stairs, and headed for the main arena. Abby, who was five, decided she'd rather watch the action from atop her daddy's lap.

I nervously fidgeted in my seat. I was concerned about Ally being down there with all the big kids. She was by far the littlest one, and I was worried—especially when I heard the announcer explain what would happen next.

"Okay, kids. Here's what you're going to do. We're going to tie a ribbon on the tail of this here goat, and you're going to chase that goat and try your best to grab that ribbon. The one who gets the ribbon first wins a Fort Worth Rodeo T-shirt and a souvenir picture. Sound good? Are you ready, cowboys and cowgirls?"

I nearly passed out.

Before I could even process all of it, they released the goat and dozens of children scattered—running, skipping, screaming, diving, giggling, and falling. I watched Ally chase after the goat, her long blond curls bouncing up and down, as we all cheered for her: "Go, Ally! You can do it!"

She pursued that goat's ribbon with great passion until her little legs got tangled up in the crowd, and she went down—face first. Our entire row gasped, afraid she was hurt. I jumped up and started to head down there, but Jeff called me back and pointed to the action. Ally was back up and running even harder after the galloping goat. Moments later, one of the older boys managed to snag the red ribbon, and the crowd stood to its feet to celebrate the boy's victory. I not only cheered for him but also for my little four-year-old who had been brave and unrelenting in her quest for the goat's ribbon. When she made it back to our seats, she was covered in dirt from head to toe.

Completely unscathed from face-planting in front of hundreds of people just minutes before, she looked up at me with a big grin and asked, "Can I do that again?"

I brushed the dirt from her blond bangs and kissed her forehead, so proud of her go-getter attitude and her ability to find joy in every situation.

I leaned over to Jeff and whispered, "Can you believe our spunky little girl? She's fearless!"

He kissed me on the cheek and whispered back, "She's you."

I loved that he thought of me in that way, but that was more than twenty years ago. I wonder if he would still say that to me today, or have I grown too comfortable in life? Have I quit chasing after dreams with the same tenacity that Ally chased after that silly goat? Have I stopped living life with that adventurous spirit? Have I stopped setting a good example for my daughters?

Have you? Are you still pursuing your passions and chasing after your goals in the midst of diapers and dishes? Or have you settled on Comfort Zone Lane, with no intention of moving anytime soon? As moms, it's easy to encourage our kids to go for their dreams. That's in our DNA. But it's not as easy to encourage ourselves to chase after our own dreams. You know, you can be a mom and still have dreams. One doesn't cancel out the other.

As I approach a big birthday this year (I won't tell you which one because I'd have to kill you, but I'm entering a whole new decade), I'm praying that I will go after every God-given dream and assignment with the same fearlessness that Ally possessed in pursuit of that goat. And I hope if I fall flat on my face, that I'll have enough spunk to get back up and keep going. And, lastly, I pray that I'll do it all with joy in my heart and the desire to do it again like my little blond spitfire.

I pray the same for you today. No matter if you're twenty-five or forty-five or you're twenty-five and feel like you're forty-five, lol, just know that God isn't through with you yet.

Bethany's JETTliner

One of the reasons I've started paying more attention to health and fitness is because my husband lost forty pounds when he was overseas. Conversely, I stress-ate forty pounds of pizza in that same time frame.

So he came home and looked amazing, and I was still carbo-loading like bread was going out of style. Justin's energy level is now through the roof, just like the three energetic boys we have.

I realized that I've lost a bit of my spunk . . . my get-up-and-go. Was I really the same girl who used to get up at 5:00 a.m. in her college days to go hang out at the lakefront just to spend a couple of hours with the guy of her dreams?

I want my kids to remember me the way I remember my younger self. I want my boys to know that I'm up for anything. My fire may have dimmed these last few years as I fell into work, deadlines, and the blessed world of pizza and burgers. But no longer.

I want my spunk back, so I'm gonna go after it.

Maybe you're in the same situation. Girlfriend, I feel ya. I hear ya. I don't want to be the tired mommy so every day I will wake up and say, "I've got this day, Lord. Help me be healthy spiritually, emotionally, and physically so I can be the best mom for my kids."

The Bible says God will give us the desire of our heart and since our bodies are a living temple of the Lord, it's time I treated mine that way.

Let's get our spunk back!

God Calls Me Renewed

Psalm 103:5 says, "He fills my life with good things. My youth is renewed like the eagle's" (NLT). He does fill our lives with good things. We're very blessed, aren't we? Just being a mother is a blessing in itself! But I also love the second part of that verse—our youth is renewed like the eagle's. Praise God! He is renewing our youth so we can have the energy to accomplish all that He has for us to do. Ask God not only to renew your youth but also to renew your dreams.

Five Ways to Boost Your Child's Confidence

If our children develop a healthy dose of self-confidence, they'll be able to go after their dreams, no matter how big or impossible they may seem. As moms, we have the opportunity to build their self-confidence every day. Here are five confidence-boosting strategies you can implement this week:

- Give each child quality time, no matter how busy you are.
- Love your children unconditionally, letting them know your love isn't based on their performance.
- Celebrate each child's uniqueness.
- Use teachable moments to develop problem-solving skills in your children.
- Be specific when praising your kids. Don't just say, "You're a good kid." Instead, say, "You're so generous. I saw you give your allowance to that homeless man today. I love your heart."

33

They Call Me Forgetful

Bethany's JETTliner

I feel like the worst mommy in the world when I forget to do something for my kids. Our children are dependent upon us for so much. If they need me to do something, it's not like they can do it for themselves.

Mommy-brain and being overwhelmed with responsibilities have cluttered my mind and while my kids are always safe, fed, and clothed, I know I drop the ball on things that are important to them.

The Bible warns against forgetfulness. Moses warns the Israelites in Deuteronomy over and over to not forget the Lord.[9] In the New Testament, believers are repeatedly encouraged to not forget the gospel message of Jesus dying, being buried, rising from the dead, and His appearances (2 Tim. 2:8). The Lord's Supper is also taught to be done in remembrance. Interestingly, Scripture talks about how offerings are signs

---

9. Tom Ascol, "The Deadly Problem of Forgetfulness," Bible Study Tools, accessed August 2, 2019, https://www.biblestudytools.com/blogs/founders-ministries-blog /forgetful-believers.html.

of God remembering His promise to us. In Genesis, the rainbow is a sign of the promise that God will remember the covenant to not destroy the earth with water again (9:12–16).

When I was in college I had an incredible mentor. We met weekly to review how things were going, and she kept a little dime store notepad where she recorded prayer requests and praises.

One Sunday night I started sharing what I'd done that week and suddenly my mentor sat up straighter and started flipping back toward the front of the notebook.

"Look," she said. "Three months ago, you were praying that you'd have opportunities to hang out with those friends." I peered at the notebook and sure enough, the three people I'd mentioned by name three months ago were the three people who had become my friends.

It seems like such a small prayer request—one that I'd actually forgotten I'd prayed, but God saw fit to listen to the inner prayers of a shy girl desperate to fit in and answered the call of her heart.

This is one of the reasons why keeping records is so important. If my mentor hadn't recalled that earlier prayer request, I would have missed an opportunity to thank God for the blessings He gives us.

It makes me wonder how many blessings I've failed to recognize.

It makes me wonder how many blessings I'm failing to help my children recognize.

Now that I'm a mom, I see myself taking on the mentor role, adding it to the many hats I wear. I need to teach my kids to remember what God does for them.

We tend to remember the bad and forget the good, but we're called to celebrate the good.

One way we do this is by keeping journals, and though my boys are not naturally inclined to write down their thoughts, I encourage it. And as for myself, I need to remember the blessings God gives us too.

So many planner systems these days have places for journaling and they've become almost like a scrapbook-calendar blend. We can print photos and paste them into the planner pages and journal a few thoughts about the day.

The Bible says to think on things that are honorable, just, pure, and lovely (Phil. 4:8 ESV). By keeping records, even just a couple of thoughts a day or a few pictures per week, we can create tangible reminders of the good.

So many times in Scripture we see God's people creating a tangible reminder of God's faithfulness with altars, like when God defeated their enemies (Exod. 17) and allowed His people to cross the Jordan River (Josh. 3–4).

Even with miraculous signs, we're a people who are prone to forget.

And when there are little ones asking for favors and begging for treats, it can be oh so easy to make promises that never get fulfilled. And despite our best efforts, we are so like the people in biblical times. So let's do our best to focus on the good things that God has done for us and remember His many blessings.

Michelle's Intel

Over the years of wearing the mama hat, I've forgotten to sign and send permission slips. I've forgotten dental appointments. I've forgotten to bake cookies for a holiday party at school and been forced to buy Oreos at the last minute, and I even forgot a parent-teacher conference once. Not my finest parenting.

But, if we're honest, we've all messed up more than we'd like to admit because there's no such thing as a perfect mom (#progressnotperfection). This is where forgetting becomes a good thing. Instead of remembering all the times you've dropped the ball, forget about them! Focus on the things you've done right! Because I can guarantee you, your kids won't remember the times you messed up. No, they'll remember how much you loved them and cared for them and wanted the very best for them. They'll remember the times you showed up and came through, and so should you. Because, Mama, you've gotten it right many more times than you've messed up.

Hebrews 8:12 says, "For I will forgive their wickedness and will remember their sins no more." Isn't that good news? Once we confess our sins to God and ask for His help in turning our lives around, He forgives and forgets. He no longer sees us as sinners. He sees us as victorious women of God doing our best to raise amazing kiddos. Why not view yourself through His eyes today? Your heavenly Father adores you. Now that's something you shouldn't forget!

God Calls Me to Remember

Psalm 77:11 says, "I will remember the deeds of the LORD; yes, I will remember your wonders of old" (ESV). We are to keep His commands and memorize Scripture so that we won't sin against Him (Ps. 119:11).

Ways to Improve Memory

1. Exercise.
2. Get enough sleep.
3. Limit or eliminate alcohol.
4. Play mental games like Sudoku or puzzles.
5. Practice meditation and relaxation techniques.

34

They Call Me Promise Keeper (but They Didn't Always . . .)

Michelle's Intel

The pile of work on my desk had grown so high that I could barely see over the top of it. Deadlines, deadlines, and more deadlines.

How am I ever going to finish all of this by next week? I wondered.

After prioritizing the stack of assignments, I took a snack break with Abby and Allyson, then ages six and four. We piled cheese atop crackers and munched until there were crumbs all over the kitchen table. It was great fun, but I had work awaiting me.

"Mommy's got to work, so I want you two to watch a movie while I get some stuff finished, okay?"

"But I thought you were going to take us to the park!" Abby protested. "You said you would. You promised!"

"Yes, I did promise, and I'll take you just as soon as I finish this one project," I negotiated. "I promise."

Abby sighed and headed for the playroom where Allyson was already absorbed in her favorite movie, *Cinderella*.

Minutes turned to hours as I worked through dinner and bath time—both handled by Daddy. Just as I put the final touches on my article, I saw a pair of green eyes peering at me over the top of my work pile.

"Whatcha doin', Ab?" I asked.

Silence.

"Did you put some of Mommy's smelly lotion on after your bath?"

Silence.

"What's wrong, sweetie?"

"You didn't take us to the park!"

"Well, Mommy didn't realize her work would take so long tonight," I explained. "But I have a good start on this work pile so I'll take you tomorrow. I promise."

"You *always promise*!" Abby said, walking away from me.

She was right. I did always promise, but I didn't always keep my promises. In fact, my mind raced as I thought back on all the promises I'd made and not kept over the past few months. Working a full-time job while trying to hit several freelance writing assignments was taking every ounce of my energy and time. I knew I had to make some changes.

I determined in my heart, that very night, I'd never again make a promise to my children I couldn't keep, and I prayed for God to help me.

The next morning, I pushed my work aside and planned a special mommy-daughter day with my girls. We shopped, ate ice cream, and visited a nearby park. No, that didn't make up for all of my broken promises, but God forgave me and so did my girls.

Of course, there have been times over the years when I've failed to keep a promise, but I've never failed to try. And, because of that, my girls have always known they could trust me.

As moms, we need to be the one person our children can count on, and that kind of trust is earned. So if we say, "I'll pick you up at three thirty at the ball field," then don't drive up at four twenty, because being late communicates two things to your child—you can't believe what I say, and you're not important in my world. Of course, those two statements are not true but if our kids think they are, the damage has already been done. Be the person whose promise means something.

If you struggle in the area of keeping promises, don't beat yourself up about it; just make a quality decision to change. It's not too late. Ask the Lord to help you in this area. He wants to help. All you have to do is ask, and He will be with you every step along the path to keeping promises. You have my word on that, and that's a promise I can keep.

Bethany's JETTliner

This devotion hits close to home because I feel like I make so many promises that I can't keep. I have the best intentions, yet sometimes circumstances make it impossible to keep those promises.

The frustrating part is that the promises I make are tiny ones, and really, they're more like suggestions. But my kids don't forget. They remember *everything*, like greedy little elephants who can't recall how to change a toilet paper roll but are adamant that six days ago I mentioned we'd grab Taco Bell for dinner.

I've learned to keep my mouth shut.

I've changed my way of thinking.

Instead of making promises, I create surprises.

If I think I'll stop for fast food after the library, I keep it to myself. If the kids are naughty, no harm, no foul, no Taco Bell for them. If they behaved, I get to surprise them with a treat and no one is upset that Mommy changed her mind (because they don't know!).

This switch in thinking has saved us money (ha ha!) and helped my reputation as a promise keeper. If I tell my boys that I'm going to take them to the gym or the pool, you better believe we're going to the gym or the pool.

If for some reason circumstances arise and we don't make it, then I'm diligent to make it up to them. As parents we have so much control over what happens in their world. My kids can't go to the pool or gym on their own so they're completely dependent on me for those fun adventures.

More importantly, I want my kids to keep their promises to me and their promises to God. How can I expect the boys to honor their word if I don't prove that I can keep mine? Furthermore, how are they to trust that God keeps *His* promises if no one in their lives demonstrates this?

Let's start today. Make surprises instead of promises, and when you do make a promise, be sure you keep it!

God Calls Me to Be Trustworthy

Proverbs 12:22 says, "The Lord detests lying lips, but he delights in people who are trustworthy." God needs us to be trustworthy so that we can be a reflection of Him. Because so many people fail to keep their word these days, it's even more important that we keep ours. Be that promise keeper in your child's life.

What to Do When You Break a Promise

So you told your son you'd play a game of Go Fish with him after you finished grading the giant stack of papers on your desk. But the grading took longer than you first thought it would, and now it's too late to play cards with your son. What should you do?

Parenting experts agree it's best to acknowledge your mistake by saying something like, "Son, I realize I messed up tonight, and I understand why you're mad at me. I had no idea it would take me so long to grade those papers. Let's reschedule our Go Fish date for three thirty tomorrow, right after school."

By apologizing and acknowledging your son's emotions, you've validated him and loved him. You may have broken your promise but you intervened in such a way that you didn't break his heart. Be mindful of the promises you make and keep them—no matter what.

35

They Call Me Best (and Worst) Listener

Bethany's JETTliner

My mom once told me that she noticed her mom always closed the book she was reading when her children got home from school. As an adult, Mom mentioned that to Grandma and she said, "The words will still be there when I open the book again."

Unfortunately, I'm guilty of not following my grandmother's example. Many times my kids have to repeat my name several times, and even though I hear them, I'm not paying attention.

Sometimes we tune our kids out. The "Mommy-Mommy-Mommyness" of it all can be drowned out by television, by kids playing, and by our own thoughts.

I'm guilty of punishing my kids for doing something I told them they could do.

I'm guilty of not being a good listener.

Thankfully, we have a God who is always listening: "For the eyes of the Lord are on the righteous, and his ears are open to their prayer" (1 Peter 3:12 ESV).

One day a friend of mine and I went "out to coffee." She brought her boys, who are older than my kids, and I was extremely impressed with their behavior. When her oldest (who was about ten years old at the time) needed her attention, he reached out and put his hand on her arm instead of calling her name or tugging on her sleeve.

My friend covered his little hand with her own. When she and I got to a stopping point in our conversation, she said, "Excuse me for a second," then she turned to him.

He had her full attention, and he'd asked for it without saying a word.

It. Was. Awesome.

We taught that little trick to our boys in steps.

Step one: When you need to interrupt Mommy (and no one is bleeding or dying), place your hand on my arm.

Step two: When I cover your hand with mine, it means, "I know you're there and I will help you as soon as I finish this part of my conversation."

Step three: I excuse myself from the conversation at the next opportunity and give you my full attention.

Game changer.

I get so engrossed in what lies beyond the computer screen that I don't pay attention to what's happening in real time with my own flesh and blood. Many times I've had to renege with my children because I don't remember agreeing to their crazy requests because they caught me when I wasn't actually listening. That builds mistrust, and I don't like it.

We've upgraded the "hand on the arm" interruption cue for when I'm on my laptop or reading. In those situations, my boys say, "Excuse me, Mommy." I nod to my child, finish my thought or get to a stopping point as quickly as I can, then turn and face them.

Eye contact is the most important thing. If I'm not looking at them, I'm not honoring them. We're in a situation where I'm with my kids 24/7. I work from home, I homeschool, and I've also learned I need to work in the same room with them or at least be in their eyeline. Creating boundaries between work time, schooltime, and playtime can be difficult.

Along with creating boundaries, there are two other pieces of boy-parenting advice that have helped our communication. The first is that boys can be listening while not maintaining eye contact. There are times when I make my boys look at me when I'm speaking to them, particularly when they're being naughty or disrespectful. However, eye contact is not required during awkward conversations like, "You've got to keep your hands out of your pockets."

The second is to touch them when you speak to them because a touch helps to center them and demonstrates positive touch associations.

I've found both to be effective.

The most important lesson is that our kids learn to be respectful but also that they know without a shadow of a doubt, we are here for them. We want our kids to tell us their innermost thoughts and share their secrets, so when they're ready to spill their guts, we need to be ready with open ears and arms.

Michelle's Intel

How many times do we shift our focus from our families to checking our email or scrolling through Instagram? Too often, I'm afraid. For that reason, I intentionally didn't have my email linked to my iPhone. That way, when I'm out and about with my husband or my daughters, I won't be distracted with the "dinging" of messages. Not having email on my phone drives some of my editors and colleagues crazy because they can't reach me right away, but I figure those messages can wait until I get home.

We are often distracted by technology when we should be focused on the person sitting right in front of us. You know, listening is almost a lost art form these days. According to facts on Transforminc.com, most of us are distracted or preoccupied about 75 percent of the time we should be listening. And, what's worse, immediately following the conversation we only remember about 50 percent of what someone told us. Bottom line? We're not very good listeners.[10]

Knowing all of that, can you think of the last time you sat down with your children or your spouse and really listened to them? Without a cell phone in your hand. Without your nose stuck in a book. Without your hands on a keyboard. I'm talking about actually focusing in on your family member and truly listening to every single word . . . how long has it been?

Make a conscious decision to listen—really listen—to your family this week. It's time we get back in the habit of making those we love—especially our children—feel important, valued, and appreciated. Listening is a great place to start.

And, while you're at it, you might want to practice listening when you pray. Prayer is two-way communication, not just you listing a bunch of prayer requests and then signing off. Try being quiet before God and listening for that still, small voice. It will change your life.

God Calls Me Heard

We serve a God who is always on call and always available. In fact, He loves our prayers. Psalm 55:16–17 says that when I call to God, He hears my voice. Paul tells us in 1 Thessalonians 5:16–17 to rejoice and pray continually, committing everything to prayer. In the same way that we

---

10. "Some Interesting Facts About Listening," Transform Inc., July 21, 2014, https://transforminc.com/2014/07/interesting-facts-listening/.

want to listen to our kids share what's going on in their worlds, our heavenly Father wants us to share with Him. We can trust that God hears us because He always keeps His promises.

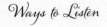

When we're super busy it can be hard to give our full attention to our kids. Here are some ways we can make our kids feel heard:

- Eat dinner together and give each child time to talk about the day.
- Turn off phones at mealtimes.
- Designate playtimes so you can have a casual conversation with your children instead of a formal discussion.
- Spend a few minutes tucking them in and ask them to share what's on their hearts.
- Be careful how you react to what your kids say. If there is a serious situation, you can deal with it, but we want our kids to know we are safe places for them to share.

36

They Call Me Blond (and Not Because That's My True Hair Color)

Michelle's Intel

We were having a slumber party at our house to celebrate Ally's twelfth birthday, so all of her closest friends piled into our SUV, and we headed to Walmart to buy their favorite snacks. (After all, you can't have a bunch of middle school girls over for a slumber party without lots of snacks.)

Stopped at the traffic light near Walmart, my eyes drifted to the empty lot across the street. Apparently, Ally's did, too, because she took one look at the tree with a "For Sale" sign on it, and said, "Like, seriously, who would buy a tree?" (Go back and say it in "Valley Girl" dialect.)

Abby, who was sitting next to me, literally slid down onto the floor-board laughing. Only Ally could think the tree was for sale and not the lot . . . bless her little blond heart. (If you're from the South, you know that's not a nice "bless your heart.")

That has become one of our family's "Favorite Ally Stories" to share. In her defense, Ally was in the gifted and talented classes at the time she made her famous "tree for sale" observation. She has always been brilliant; she just has blond moments from time to time. But hey, who doesn't?

I know I can relate.

A couple of Christmas Eves ago, I had a bit of a blond moment myself. You see, several of us had asked for Fitbits for Christmas, and Nana let us open them on Christmas Eve so we could set them up together and start using them right away. Ally and her then fiancé (now hubby), Wesley, opened theirs, and I opened mine. Reading through the instructions together, we carefully followed all of the setup steps. Right away, Ally's and Wesley's Fitbits started working, but mine wouldn't cooperate. I ran through the steps again . . . still nothing.

Frustrated that mine was broken, I sighed.

"I guess I'll have to wait in that crazy return line the day after Christmas with the rest of humanity and see if I can exchange it for a Fitbit that actually works."

"What exactly is wrong with yours?" Wesley asked.

"Well, I set the time like three times, and it won't budge," I said, showing him. "See? It's stuck on twelve."

He looked at me the same way I'd looked at Ally all those years ago, sitting at that stoplight near Walmart. Then he reached down and peeled off the sticker from the top of my Fitbit—the sticker that said "12:00" on it.

The whole family laughed for a good twenty minutes. I still think it was an honest mistake. At any rate, the Fitbit story goes in the "Favorite Mom Stories" folder.

Truth is, we all have blond moments every once in a while. They're no indication of our intellectual capabilities; they simply show that even the smartest people make stupid and often really funny mistakes. If you can laugh at yourself, you won't mind those blond moments nearly as much.

Inside jokes and blond moments are what favorite, funny, family memories are made of. They bond you together forever, and they never fail to make you laugh. I bet your family has its own blond moments memory file; am I right? (You're thinking of a doozy right now, aren't you?)

As part of the family of God, don't you wonder if God has a "Favorite Funny Stories" folder on each of us? It wouldn't surprise me a bit if He did. After all, He is the one who gave us the ability to laugh. He is the one who fills us with joy! He wants us to enjoy life.

So, if you've been a "Sober Sally" lately, lighten up! Share a funny story or two with your kids or pull out the old family movies and laugh your way through your kids' cutest footage.

And don't stress out the next time you have a blond moment. Just think of it as more material for your funny family folder.

Bethany's JETTliner

My boys have reached the age where they like to tease me, so if I mess up saying *anything*, they erupt into laughter. Even if they misheard me, I still get teased, though I didn't say anything wrong. It's okay, because I've been collecting stories on them for years (insert semi-evil mommy laugh).

Instead of getting upset, I just laugh with them. It's hard to tease someone who thinks their mistake is funny, which is a lesson we teach the boys. They're going to do something embarrassing at some point, but if they laugh at themselves, there's no foothold for kids to be mean. However, if one of the boys says or does something silly and the others start teasing too much, it's my responsibility to step in and draw the line. Playful teasing is one thing but meanness is another.

Having a healthy sense of humor is a great characteristic to pass on to your kids, so the next time they tease you about something, laugh it off and smile.

God Calls Me Delightful

Psalm 149:4 says, "For the LORD delights in his people" (NLT). Did you get that? The King of Kings delights in you! And Psalm 2:4 says, "In heaven the LORD laughs as he sits on his throne" (CEV) in reference to the nations that mock Him. I love that it says, "He laughs." I like to think He is sitting on His throne, enjoying a good laugh, whenever we have a blond moment. There will be lots of laughter in heaven, so you better get used to it! If you haven't giggled with your kids in a while, bust out a belly laugh today!

Funny Family Videos

If I have one regret, it's that I never took time to interview my parents on camera before they went to heaven. They had the funniest stories—stories my siblings and I can't remember exactly. But just because I missed my opportunity doesn't mean you have to, right? So why don't you and your kiddos shoot your own "Family Funnies" movie?

You could even do this using your smartphone, or if your loved ones live miles away, you can use Zoom to record your interviews. Be creative and ask questions such as: "What's the funniest thing that ever happened to you? What's your favorite funny family memory? Did you ever laugh so hard your sides actually hurt? Tell me about that . . ."

Then, put all the footage together with some nice roll-in music and fancy editing, and show your funny family feature film at your next get-together or save it for the holidays and break it out on Christmas Eve. The gift of family history and laughter . . . what could be better?

37

They Call Me Bargain Shopper

Bethany's JETTliner

Now that the boys are hitting growth spurts, they're eating everything in sight. The grocery bill will continue to climb as they enter the teen years, so we're teaching the boys how to handle a food budget. Instead of treating them to Menchie's Frozen Yogurt, which charges you based on the weight of your treat, we challenged them to see if they could spend less and get more at the grocery store.

Justin and I set the budget at fifteen dollars, which included sales tax. Then we helped the boys create their shopping list based on what they would choose at the froyo shop.

Since Menchie's charges per ounce, the boys aren't allowed to get "bottom-ers," which are donuts or cakes that sit underneath the frozen yogurt and add considerable weight to their treat. However, since we were buying "in bulk" at Publix, a bottom-er could be purchased.

With their agreed-upon donuts, we moved to the topping stage, leaving the ice cream for last so it wouldn't melt. The candy aisle held many treats, including maraschino cherries. Eagerly they placed the glass jar in the cart, excited to have more than two on top of their ice cream. Publix brand candy at ninety-nine cents per bag fit their budget so they each picked out a favorite.

We added up their purchases thus far and headed to the ice cream. Justin explained how the buy-one-get-one deals worked, and luckily, there were brands with two-for-one offers. Once we helped three boys choose two flavors to share, we conducted a mini-homeschool math session in the frozen food aisle. Satisfied the items in the cart were under budget, we marched to the checkout, and the boys eyeballed the numbers that appeared on the cash register: $14.79.

Success!

Not only had the boys stayed under their budget, but also all of us enjoyed ice cream and toppings (and bottom-ers!) with plenty left over. It cost us less than Menchie's and the boys loved their giant scoops.

Being prudent with money is a biblical skill. In Matthew 25, we explore the parable of the talents. Each steward is responsible for creating a return on the money the master gave to him. Each was rewarded based on his effort, except for the man who buried the talent and did nothing.

In a similar regard, money not spent is a lot like money earned. If we budget thirty dollars for frozen yogurt but get all the ingredients for fifteen dollars, that is fifteen dollars left to save or spend. As part of our goal to teach our children to be good stewards of their resources, we opened checking accounts for each child so the boys can learn from an early age a healthy relationship with money and material items.

A second lesson we teach our kids is how to flip items they find at garage sales or thrift stores. We research items they find to see what they're selling for online before making their purchases. Once an item is in hand, they'll photograph it and my husband will upload it to eBay,

Craigslist, or Facebook Marketplace on their behalf. This flip method is a fantastic way to teach kids to pay attention to the marketplace and how to quickly make a profit.

And with that profit, we teach our children to be generous, to love others, and to give back. Not only is this a life lesson and a heart lesson for kids, this principle reinforces my own (sometimes not-so-healthy) relationship with money and allows me to grow as well.

Michelle's Intel

I've never met a sale I didn't like, and my daughters are the same way. We are bona fide bargain shoppers. And since we've had a lot of practice bargain hunting over the years, we are pretty skilled when it comes to getting amazing deals. One way we use our skills to bless others is by picking up extra on-sale supplies for various charities in our community.

For example, I know our local humane society always needs bleach, paper towels, laundry detergent, dog and cat toys, kitty litter, and towels. If I happen to see a good deal on any of those items, I'll purchase some extra and drop them off at the White River Humane Society.

I also learned recently that a nearby women's shelter loves receiving cake mixes, icing, and candles, so that moms who are living there with their children can bake birthday cakes for their kiddos. So you can bet I'm on the lookout for sales on those party items. When I stockpile enough, I'll drop them off at the women's shelter.

Another way to be a blessing? When school supplies go on sale, treat your children's teachers with markers, crayons, tissues, pens, hand lotion, or scented antibacterial gel. Teachers often spend their own money on supplies, so why not be a blessing?

The Bible says, "Do not withhold good from those to whom it is due, when it is in your power to act" (Prov. 3:27). So, put those smart shopping skills to good use. You'll not only be teaching your children how to find bargains, you'll also be teaching them how to be a blessing. It's a win-win!

God Calls Me Priceless

On days when we feel like we're worthless or totally failing at life, God reminds us that we are priceless to Him. We were bought with a price . . . a price so high that it cost Jesus His life (1 Cor. 6:20). We mean more to God than we will ever know.

Flip Challenge

Teach your children to buy and sell by looking for deals at garage sales or thrift stores.

- Start them off with ten dollars.
- Use checkbook registers to monitor their progress.
- Make it a fun competition by seeing who makes the most profit after a certain period of time.

38

They Call Me Out

Michelle's Intel

"Ab, honey, are you okay?" I asked, sitting on the edge of her bed.
She nodded, but I could see my then ten-year-old had been crying.

Abby wasn't talking but thankfully, her little sister was. Allyson confirmed what my mama's heart already knew to be true; Abby's two best friends had left her out . . . again.

I just couldn't understand why these two little girls continued to hurt my daughter. Why wouldn't they just include her in their plans? Would it really kill them to ask Abby to go with them to the movies?

Thinking quickly, I came up with a surefire plan to mend Abby's hurting heart, or at least take her mind off of it for the night.

"Abby, let's go pick out your birthday invitations," I suggested. "We can plan your whole party! Sound like fun?"

"Yeah," she answered with just a hint of a smile.

As we combed the aisles of the giant party store, I could see the light coming back into Ab's eyes. She and Ally tried on silly hats and pranced around in feather boas before settling on a Hollywood theme.

Back home, we popped popcorn, put on a Disney movie, and began writing the invitations so we could mail them the following morning.

As we compiled the guest list, I was surprised when Abby rattled off the names of those two girls who had deliberately excluded her from their weekend plans.

"Are you sure you want to invite them to your party?" I asked. "I mean, they aren't very nice to you, and you have lots of other friends. You don't need them at your party."

Without missing a beat, Abby said, "I know . . . but I don't want to leave them out and hurt their feelings . . . because I know how that feels. Can I invite them, Mommy?"

"Of course," I answered.

In that moment, I realized that just because I wear the official mom hat, that hat certainly didn't make me right all the time. In fact, I wanted to pull that mom hat over my face and hide for a bit. Instead, I asked God to forgive me, and I thanked Him for Abby and Ally—my sweet little girls with very big hearts.

As I've been working on this book, I've been reflecting on how much I have learned from my children over the years, and how much I've gleaned from them recently.

I bet you feel the same about your kiddos.

Psalm 127:3 says, "Children are a gift from the LORD; they are a reward from him" (NLT), and I'd have to agree. Not only do we enjoy them, but also they make us want to be better people. When I see Abby going the extra mile for a coworker who hasn't been especially nice to her I'm inspired to be better. And when I'm following Ally in my car and I see her pull over and hand a homeless man money and a bottle of water, I want to be better.

I want to be more like them because I see them being more like Jesus.

I know I am biased, but I'm also blessed beyond measure to have two daughters who teach me to be better, simply by watching them do life.

So here's my #momchallenge for you this week. Really observe your children and make note of the times they inspire you. You'll not only want to share those instances with your kiddos someday, but also, you'll want to review them on the days your children aren't so inspiring, lol.

Aren't you glad that teachable moments go both ways, and aren't you grateful that we can grow up, spiritually speaking, right alongside our children?

Bethany's JETTliner

"That's a naughty word, Mommy."

I glanced at my then six-year-old. "What word, baby?"

He leaned forward and whispered, "The bad word."

I realized he was listening to the television show that was playing while I cooked dinner. I'd tuned out the TV so I wasn't sure what word he'd heard.

"Can you tell Mommy so I know?"

He nodded and whispered again, "Stupid."

I hugged him tight, relieved that *stupid* was the word that came out of his mouth. "That is a naughty word, baby. Thanks for letting me know." I turned off the television. Satisfied, he ran off to play with his brothers.

More recently, I had a reality cooking show playing in the background. "What are all those noises for?" asked my son.

"They're bleeping out his bad words," I said.

"He's saying a lot of bad words. We aren't supposed to say bad words."

Yup. He *was* saying a lot of bad words—words that were worse than *stupid*, that's for sure. By letting the show play, bleeped-out words or not, I wasn't setting a good example for my kids. I'd become desensitized.

The words I was letting the television bleep (and some that weren't bleeped) were not words that are allowed in our house and definitely aren't words that we say to one another.

The Holy Spirit convicts us of our sin: "When he comes, he will convict the world concerning sin and righteousness" (John 16:8 ESV). Sometimes it's words out of the mouths of babes that God will use to convict us.

Let us always be willing to hear and learn from our children so that we may be more like Jesus.

God Calls Me Being Transformed

Second Corinthians 3:18 says, "And we all, who with unveiled faces contemplate the Lord's glory, are being transformed into his image with ever-increasing glory, which comes from the Lord, who is the Spirit." Isn't it great that God still loves us and believes in us while we're being transformed? That's very good news to me. I'm part of the lifelong learners club, and I'm thankful our heavenly Father is patient with me while I'm going through the process of becoming better. How about you?

Six Things Children Teach Us About Life

While taking pictures at my grandson Bear's first birthday party a few weeks ago, I was almost moved to tears as I observed another little toddler comforting Bear.

The cake had been eaten. The toys unwrapped. The guests were starting to file out. The afternoon was almost over, and Bear was D-O-N-E, done. But his mama wanted a picture with him and a former co-teacher and her little boy; however, Bear wasn't having it. He started wailing, with real tears, and the little boy in the other mama's arms leaned over and gave Bear a big ole kiss on the head. He was desperately trying to comfort Baby Bear.

I loved that.

It reminded me just how much we can learn from our littles, such as learning to do these:

- Show empathy.
- Slow down.
- Find wonder in everyday things.
- Connect with others.
- Forgive easily.
- Ask questions.

39

They Call Me Advocate

Bethany's JETTliner

We are naturally protective of our kids but learning to advocate is a skill that we grow and develop. Sometimes we have to squash the anger that bubbles up in our bellies to be more effective on our children's behalf. And sometimes, when our children are being hurt, we have to unleash the fury inside. Knowing the difference and the appropriate time for each comes with wisdom and experience.

But when you're in the thick of making a decision, the crossroads in front of you come with pros and cons laced with mom guilt and worry.

When my littlest went to school for the first time, I expected him to have so much fun coloring, learning, and playing with other kids his age. This was not the case. His experience turned sour when he was assigned to a teacher who never should have been teaching little ones. She yelled constantly—even at the open house. I knew this was not a good situation.

Red flag.

My son's stomach hurt every morning before school and he cried every night when he got home. His homework and assignments created an extreme anxiety and tension if he didn't do exactly what he thought his teacher wanted, down to how he wrote the date on his paper.

Red flag.

I reached out to the administration but they refused to move my son into a different classroom.

Red flag.

What was I supposed to do? I felt powerless in a system that begs for parental involvement but punishes the parents who advocate when it doesn't fit the model.

On the one hand, I wanted my son to know that I would always stand up for him, that I would use my voice when he couldn't.

On the other hand, perhaps this was an opportunity to teach my son coping skills for dealing with difficult people.

And while I did not have a clear answer on which was the right path, I stayed the course and prayed constantly for a change in his situation.

Then God gave me the opportunity to see firsthand what was happening in the classroom.

I guest taught his class for the Great American Teach-In and watched my confident little boy sit ramrod straight in his chair, afraid to move or raise his hand. When I needed volunteers to help hold my visual aids, my son and some of his classmates helped, but my son's wide eyes were constantly on his teacher and he moved with rigid motions.

Flag on fire.

I'd had it.

I couldn't put him through another several months of this behavior. Even though I was in the middle of starting up two businesses, we withdrew him and went back to homeschooling.

And never looked back.

Sometimes our kids need us to advocate on their behalf for more than a negative school situation.

Lacey Buchanan's son Christian was born with Tessier Cleft Palate, an extremely rare birth defect. He required numerous surgeries as an infant. When the insurance companies dictated Christian's care, Lacey stepped in and fought. Throughout her journey as a parent of a child with special needs, Lacey's confidence grew and she became Christian's voice. By the grace of God, the best doctors were finally able to take Christian as their patient. Lacey continues to be an advocate for him and others who are in a similar situation.

Similarly, my sister Jill grew into her role as caregiver and advocate for her daughter when KP was diagnosed with severe hip dysplasia. Jill's husband was traveling for work for many months during the time of the major surgery, and Jill bravely became the voice for her "little pink hipster."

In the same way that we speak up for our kids, Jesus speaks up for us. It's by God's grace only that we receive salvation and it is Jesus who stands in our place and advocates on our behalf.

Likewise, the Holy Spirit is our advocate. Scripture says that even when we don't know what to pray, the Holy Spirit utters groans that words cannot express (Rom. 8:26–27). The Spirit helps us in our weakness and the Lord knows that we moms have many epic fail moments.

At the end of the day, our kids need to know that we have their backs and that while we teach them to stand up for themselves, we're there to stand up for them.

Michelle's Intel

Knowing when to step in and when to step back is one of the hardest things to learn on this parenting journey—at least it has been for me. While we want our children to learn to fight their own battles, sometimes their battles are too big, and they are too little. Until our children find their voice, we must be that voice for them.

When Abby was in third grade, she started struggling in her studies. I had a parent-teacher conference with her homeroom teacher who whispered to me, "Abby is smart but she's having trouble reading, and since every worksheet we do involves reading of some sort, she is falling way behind."

I died a little inside. Mom guilt overwhelmed me.

Maybe I hadn't worked with her enough. Maybe I should've ordered her that Hooked on Phonics set I saw on TV last week. Maybe this is my fault.

She continued, "Our school system won't pay to have Abby tested for light sensitivity but you should. I think that might be her issue."

I started to go into the office and demand they test Abby for light sensitivity, but instead, I called Sylvan Learning Center. Sure enough, one afternoon of testing confirmed what Abby's teacher believed to be true—Abby suffered from a disorder known as Irlen syndrome. Basically, she couldn't track black text on white paper. The words would appear to move, and she'd get headaches when trying to read or do math. Everything looked distorted to Ab, so she would simply stop trying.

The solution was so simple. Before Abby could do her worksheets, she had to place a lavender-colored acetate sheet over the white paper. Immediately, her grades improved and she never looked back.

I, however, had to fight for Abby to be able to retake many of the tests she'd already taken and failed up until we discovered her light sensitivity, because her grades didn't reflect her level of comprehension. One battle at a time, Abby was able to retake her tests and came out of third grade an A/B student.

Looking back, I'm so thankful for Abby's third grade homeroom teacher. She cared enough to do something for my child. She took it as far as she could and then handed the baton to me. I had Abby's back, but

God had mine. He has yours too. Don't be afraid to stand up for your children. This is more than being a Mama Bear. This is about getting involved and fighting for your children and other mamas' kids when needed—like Abby's third grade teacher did for her. They're counting on us.

God Calls Me to Advocate

God is serious about advocacy. Over and over in Scripture He tells us to take care of others and to care for the orphans and widows. Psalm 41:1 says, "Blessed are those who have regard for the weak; the LORD delivers them in times of trouble." In Isaiah 1:17 we read, "Learn to do right; seek justice. Defend the oppressed. Take up the cause of the fatherless; plead the case of the widow."

Loving God means loving others. We must advocate for our children and for those who don't have a strong voice. May God open our eyes to see how we can help others, and may He give us strength to stand up for those who need help.

How You Can Be an Effective Advocate

- Know the information. Be informed. Stay up-to-date with the news around your issue.
- Network. Who are the major players in the field? Whom are others listening to?
- Get involved. Volunteer or help in any way you can.
- Understand the terminology. Each field has its own lingo. Be sure you're using the proper terms so you don't offend those you're trying to help.

40

They Call Me Silver-Lining Finder

Michelle's Intel

We were all in shock over Nana's passing. I was sure Jeff's mama would outlive us all. She certainly didn't look eighty-three, and she didn't act her age either. In fact, Martha still worked three days a week up until she went into the hospital with what we thought was a gallbladder attack.

It turned out to be much more.

While Jeff stayed with his mama in Indiana, trying to get answers from a team of doctors about her declining health, I stayed by Abby's bedside in a hospital in Lexington, Kentucky, as she battled preeclampsia complications. It seemed our grandson would arrive earlier than expected.

It was a crazy month. Baby Bear had to remain in the NICU until he could breathe and eat on his own, and Abby had to stay in the hospital until her blood pressure stabilized. On the very day they were both released, we got word that Nana had taken a turn for the worse. We all headed to Indianapolis, hopeful she would recover but very much aware she might not.

That next night, I looked around the critical care waiting room at my two sweet daughters, their amazing husbands, my adorable new grand-baby, and my precious husband, and I was overwhelmed with emotion. Though it was a terrible situation, I was thankful we could all be together.

We passed the hours, sharing funny stories about Nana and taking turns holding Baby Bear. And though Nana had already slipped into an unconscious state, we introduced her to her great-grandson and told her how much we loved her before saying our final goodbyes.

It was a very sad time for our family, yet in the midst of loss, we found comfort in our God, and hope in the face of sweet Baby Bear.

We found our silver lining.

As moms, we can't protect our children from disappointment and loss any more than we can protect ourselves. But we can do three things. We can be there for our children as they walk through grief and deal with disappointments, letting them vent, cry, and try to make sense of it all. We can pray with them and for them as they grieve and find a new normal. And we can be the silver-lining finder. In other words, we can always look for something to be thankful for, even when dark clouds seem to blanket the sky.

I don't know what your family is facing today, but I do know this: you don't have to face it alone. God will carry you when you can't stand on your own, and He will help you be the mom you need to be in the midst of troubled times. Allow yourself time to grieve, but also make it your mission to find the silver lining, and then share that discovery with your children. I'm not suggesting you be the Pollyanna of the family, but I am suggesting you bring light to a dark situation. By finding that silver lining, you have the power to bring hope to your hurting kiddos.

There's just something about a mother's touch. When you're sick or when things take a turn for the worse, we always want our moms, no matter how old we are. What a privilege to be that go-to person for our children. That's sort of a silver lining in itself, isn't it?

Bethany's JETTliner

My kids were both happy and unhappy when we pulled them out of school. We'd homeschooled for two years and thought we'd found a great learning environment for them just five minutes away from home.

But reality set in, and Justin and I both knew that school was not a good situation for any of the three boys. So the week before Christmas break, I filled out the paperwork, withdrew the boys, and kissed the school goodbye.

While not heartbroken over the lack of schoolwork, the boys were extremely sad that they couldn't see their friends anymore. They missed sharing Pokémon cards in the cafeteria and sitting with their besties at lunch. However, I knew in my soul that homeschool was again the right option, so I had to find the silver lining for them because they couldn't see it for themselves.

"Guess what, boys!" I said on our first official homeschool day after the holidays. "You didn't have to wake up at six a.m. today! And once you get all your work for the day completed, we can go to the pool."

The boys cheered.

While they still missed their friends, Justin and I made sure to get excited about the friends they met at church and we encouraged them to play with the neighborhood kids before dinner. We've met other homeschool families through co-ops and online, so our kids are able to text and play with each other virtually . . . even sharing in one another's birthday party events from hundreds of miles away.

Sometimes we have to make hard decisions as parents, but if we look for the positives, we can make hard situations easier and help our kids learn to have positive attitudes despite their circumstances.

God Calls Me to Be Thankful

Psalm 50:23 says, "But giving thanks is a sacrifice that truly honors me" (NLT). When we praise God, we bring Him on the scene. In fact, the Word says he inhabits the praises of His people (Ps. 22:3 NKJV). So, when your family is facing difficult situations, when you feel the least like praising God, that's when you should offer up thanksgiving. I know it doesn't seem to make any sense, but God's ways are higher than our ways. Praise changes the atmosphere, so get your praise on, and encourage your kids to do the same!

Silver Linings in the Word of God

No matter what you're facing today, the Bible is filled with silver-lining Scriptures. Isn't that good news? I thought I'd list a few so you could read them with your children during those not-so-sunny seasons of life.

- If you're feeling discouraged: "'For I know the plans I have for you,' declares the LORD, 'plans to prosper you and not to harm you, plans to give you hope and a future'" (Jer. 29:11).

- If you're feeling weak and helpless: "But he said to me, 'My grace is sufficient for you, for my power is made perfect in weakness.' Therefore I will boast all the more gladly about my weaknesses, so that Christ's power may rest on me" (2 Cor. 12:9).

- If you're feeling stressed: "Trust in the LORD with all your heart; do not depend on your own understanding" (Prov. 3:5 NLT).

- If you're feeling afraid: "They do not fear bad news; they confidently trust the LORD to care for them" (Ps. 112:7 NLT).

- If you're feeling anxious: "Do not be anxious about anything, but in every situation, by prayer and petition, with thanksgiving, present your requests to God. And the peace of God, which transcends all understanding, will guard your hearts and your minds in Christ Jesus" (Phil. 4:6–7).

- If you're feeling sad: "I waited patiently for the LORD; he turned to me and heard my cry. He lifted me out of the slimy pit, out of the mud and mire; he set my feet on a rock and gave me a firm place to stand. He put a new song in my mouth, a hymn of praise to our God. Many will see and fear the LORD and put their trust in him" (Ps. 40:1–3).

41

They Call Me Referee

Bethany's JETTliner

"I'm telling!"

I've never hated two words more in my entire life. When the nasally singsong threat rings out, I want to hide under a table or steer the offended child to his daddy.

When the boys were little, tattling was a nuisance. Now that they're older, tattling is survival.

I encourage the boys to tattle because the tattle happens *before* the boys break out the fisticuffs.

Separating three wrestling boys is not my idea of a good time and yet it seems like they have made it my life's work to be the referee. With three kids, there are always two who are picking at each other.

Wearing the referee hat is exhausting. The tattling interruptions break the rhythm of our work and our train of thought. And the thing is, the tattling is 99 percent over something really stupid.

"He threw my Lego sword."

"He turned the light off."

"He took my Pokémon."

Being the referee is emotionally draining because sometimes the answer is not as cut-and-dried as "Give it back." Sometimes the situation requires a parent to step in and resolve the issue.

This is the time to teach our kids objectivity. These tattle-telling episodes will always happen at the most inconvenient time for you, but the Bible says in Deuteronomy 11:19 to teach the Word of God at all times, when you sit at home and when you walk along the road. I wish I could add "and when you're right in the middle of filing your taxes and when you're on a deadline," but the Bible doesn't work like that.

The best thing we can do is take a deep breath and take advantage of the opportunity presented. Both children are offended by the other, so this is a good time to have one child express why he or she is upset while the other child patiently waits a turn without interrupting.

Our kids will not do this perfectly. Patience is hard, particularly when you don't agree with the other person. But teaching our kids objectivity, empathy, and interpersonal communication skills sets them up to be a mature adult. Most kids don't want to understand each other's point of view so we have to point it out.

Today my middle son complained that his brothers never want to play video games with him despite the hours they played together this morning. "You're mean to them," I said. "You got mad and threw a fit. No one wants to play with someone who acts like that."

Similarly, God is the referee when I throw an internal fit: "No one wants to work with someone who has a bad attitude, Bethany. You need to work on forgiveness." The wonderful thing about God is that if you ask Him to open your eyes to your sin, He will. Unfortunately, our kids probably won't ask us to point out where they can make improvements in their behavior. By humbling ourselves to Jesus, we can lead our kids by example. The next time we want to throw a fit, we can verbalize our feelings and demonstrate how to work things out with love and kindness.

Michelle's Intel

Black and white is my favorite color combination, but I never have enjoyed wearing a referee shirt. When my girls were little, they knew if either one of them tattled, both of them were probably going to be grounded. This understanding, based on past experience, cut way down on the tattling in our household.

But once in a while, this tactic worked *too* well, because I couldn't find out who committed the disobedient act, and neither of them would talk.

One such time involved a big wad of chewing gum stuck under the leather back seat of my new Ford Explorer.

"Who did it?" I asked, staring at them in the rearview mirror.

Silence.

"I'm going to ask you one more time . . . who stuck the big wad of gum under the seat?"

Still no one said a word.

It was time to break out the big guns.

"You know, Mommy used to be a police beat reporter for the newspaper and I still have a lot of friends in law enforcement, so you leave me no choice. I'm going to take that wad of gum down to the police station and have them test it for DNA. I should have the results by Friday, and I'll know which of you did it."

Their eyes were huge. It was working, so I continued.

"Furthermore, whichever one of you did it will get in trouble for the original act and will suffer a second punishment for withholding the information. That's two punishments."

We hadn't even made it out of the driveway before Abby began sobbing, "I did it, Mommy. I did it. Just give me one punishment, pleaaaaassse! Just one, Mommy."

Case solved.

While I appreciated their solidarity, I needed to know the truth. And don't worry about Ab. She didn't get in too much trouble. But she did lose gum privileges for a very long time.

It's important that our children know there are consequences for their actions, but it's equally important that they know they can trust us to be fair with them. That's why I didn't come down too hard on Abby.

I've learned when I wrap my disciplinary actions in mercy and love, I rarely go wrong.

God Calls Me Understood

A referee must have full knowledge of the rules of a game and all of the possible exceptions. They must be trained on what to watch for and where any cheating or unsportsmanlike conduct could occur. Hebrews 4:15 says, "We do not have a high priest who is unable to empathize with our weaknesses, but we have one who has been tempted in every way, just as we are—yet he did not sin." Jesus knows exactly what to look for in our hearts because He experienced every emotion we experience. Since He was perfect, we can trust that God truly understands us and loves us in spite of ourselves.

How to Keep Your Sanity When Your Kids Act Crazy

- Take a deep breath.
- Pray and ask God for strength.

- Excuse yourself from the room if you need a moment to calm down.
- Make the children go to separate rooms.
- Turn off any noisemaking appliances like the radio or television.
- Institute mandatory rest time.
- Have your kids run a few laps outside to burn off excess energy.
- Drink some coffee (or in Michelle's case, a Polar Pop cup full of Diet Pepsi).

42

They Call Me in the Middle of the Night

Michelle's Intel

It's automatic. It's almost instinctive. As moms, when we hear our child's voice calling for us, we jump into action. It doesn't matter if it's the middle of the night, we are on it! But do we do the same when God calls for us in the middle of the night? Or do we simply roll over and go back to sleep, convincing ourselves we didn't really hear from Him? As a mother, I've had times when the Lord has prompted me to pray for one or both of my daughters, though at those exact moments, I had no idea why. I'll simply wake up at 3:00 a.m. with an intense urgency to pray for Abby or Allyson, and I'll pray until I feel peace, and then I'll go back to sleep. Has this ever happened to you?

I've found God doesn't always reveal why He calls us to pray. Sometimes we never know. And sometimes we find out later. But that's not what's important. What's important is that, as moms, we're obedient to the call.

During the time Allyson was in LA studying at the Fashion Institute of Design & Merchandising, we were in constant contact. She was barely eighteen when we moved her to the City of Angels, and this mama was more than a little nervous about the whole thing. With my baby girl more than two thousand miles away, I became even more sensitive to the Lord's wake-up calls.

I had one of those divine wake-up calls during Ally's second year in LA. I sat straight up in bed, grabbed my phone from the nightstand to check the time, and started praying for Allyson. It was 12:27 a.m. Indiana time, so it was 9:27 p.m. in LA. I had no idea what was going on with Ally, but I knew I needed to pray. I reached across the bed and shook Jeff awake, asking him to pray too. Moments later, both our cell phones vibrated.

It was Ally.

"Are you guys awake?" she texted.

I called her immediately and learned why God had awakened us. That night after Ally's class ended, she headed toward her apartment just like always, but this time, a homeless man who was high on something grabbed Ally's hair and tried to pull her to the ground. But thankfully, an off-duty policeman saw the whole thing happen and intervened just in time. He pulled Ally into a nearby Walgreens and stayed with her until an Uber arrived to take her back to her apartment. Allyson was quite shaken but she was also thankful that God had provided a way of escape for her.

And so were we.

I'm so thankful God cares about our children even more than we do. And I'm so grateful the Word says He never slumbers so we can rest assured God is watching over our children even when we can't.

As mothers, we are that first line of prayer defense for our kiddos. With everything we do for our children—from being their taxi drivers to fixing their meals to doing their laundry to helping with their homework—

nothing is more important than covering them with prayer. Go ahead. Get your prayer on! It's not only our job; it's our greatest privilege.

Bethany's JETTliner

"You call us if you need us, baby," I told my son. "We'll come get you." My husband and I gave him big hugs and kisses and walked with him to the front door of his friend's house. At age six, he was having his very first sleepover and I was a nervous wreck.

He knocked on the door and proudly entered our friends' home. "Bye, Mommy. Bye, Daddy," he said, and with a wave, he was off to his playmate's room.

"Just call us if he needs us," we told our friend, and then we left our baby for the night.

Around two in the morning, the phone rang.

"He wants to come home," my friend said. "I've been rocking with him but he won't fall back asleep."

I was awake in an instant.

"I'm on my way."

Luckily our friend didn't live far away, but I would have driven any distance to get my child. I pulled in the driveway, left the car running, and dimmed the headlights. My friend was waiting for us inside, so I didn't have to knock. She opened the door and handed me his backpack. I slung it over my shoulder and scooped my little boy into my arms.

"Mommy's here," I whispered as he burrowed his face into my neck. I thanked my friend, then buckled my sweetheart into the car. "I'll always come get you," I told him.

And I always will.

No matter how far, no matter what's happening, if my kids need me at 1:00 p.m. or 1:00 a.m., I will be there.

God will be there too. It doesn't matter what time it is or what is happening. We can trust that we are so valuable and important to Him that if we call His name, He's ready to catch us and make us feel safe.

God Calls Me Intercessor

First Timothy 2:1 says, "I urge you, first of all, to pray for all people. Ask God to help them; intercede on their behalf, and give thanks for them" (NLT). What an honor to have the Creator of the universe call on us to pray! You see, sometimes He has us pray for our children, and sometimes He wakes us up to pray for someone else's child. Be obedient. Be faithful. And pray like somebody's life is on the line because it just might be.

Five Scriptures to Pray Over Your Children

"And I am certain that God, who began the good work within you, will continue his work until it is finally finished on the day when Christ Jesus returns" (Phil. 1:6 NLT).

"The LORD directs the steps of the godly. He delights in every detail of their lives" (Ps. 37:23 NLT).

"I pray that your love will overflow more and more, and that you will keep on growing in knowledge and understanding" (Phil. 1:9 NLT).

"But grow in the grace and knowledge of our Lord and Savior Jesus Christ. To him be glory both now and forever! Amen" (2 Peter 3:18).

"For God has not given us a spirit of fear, but of power and of love and of a sound mind" (2 Tim. 1:7 NKJV).

43

They Call Me Safe Zone

Bethany's JETTliner

Deep belly laughs followed by shrieks and the thud of heavy footsteps across the carpet mean only one thing: Daddy is chasing.

Suddenly my youngest sweeps into my bedroom, rounds the corners of the bed, and grabs for me. My husband is close behind and Josiah yells, "Mommy is the Safe Zone! Mommy is the Safe Zone!"

I lean down and wrap my arm around him.

I l-o-v-e being the safe zone.

Daddy respects the invisible force field now protecting my baby from his tickling fingers and I'm instantly transported back to when my boys were toddlers.

"Mommies are safe!" was the battle cry of the day. The boys would snuggle into my arms, hide their faces, then slowly peek around to see where Daddy was lurking before waddling out of the room as fast as they could.

Mothers have an instinctual need to keep their young safe, even if it's just to give them a break from a wrestling match or tickle time. Even animal parents demonstrate this inclination. Cheetahs move their babies every few days to remove any scent trails.[11] Strawberry poison dart frog mothers will move their babies individually into separate waters so the tadpole siblings don't eat each other, and the daddy frog pees on the babies to keep them from drying out.[12]

Beyond protecting our kids (and hopefully not peeing on them), we have eighteen years to prove to them that we are their safe place.

One thing I teach my kids is that no matter what they do or how badly they mess up, I will always love them. That no matter what they do, *God* will always love them.

The disappointment level dips but the love never does.

This message is verbally repeated to them when they're in trouble, but beyond saying the words, I have to prove it's true with my actions. I can't hold a grudge if I'm upset with them and I can't throw their mistakes in their faces.

This past weekend my oldest son was on an overnight youth retreat. The group was scheduled to arrive home around eleven on Saturday night. At nine thirty I received a text from the youth minister's wife. My son lost his phone and they had gone back to the conference center to find it.

I knew my son, who is one of the youngest on the trip, had to be mortified.

"Oh wow. I'm sorry that's making you guys late coming home," I texted. "I know he must feel terrible and we do too."

Thankfully the phone was turned in to security, but not until an hour

---

11. "5 Remarkable Animal Moms," World Wildlife Fund, accessed August 2, 2019, https://www.worldwildlife.org/stories/5-remarkable-animal-moms.

12. Michelle Douglass, "10 Astonishing Animal Parents," BBC Earth, July 23, 2015, http://www.bbc.com/earth/story/20150723-10-astonishing-animal-parents.

later and by that time, our youth group was almost back to Tampa. When he got into the car, I asked him about losing his phone.

"Did you feel embarrassed?" I asked.

"Yes, I felt terrible," he said as he buckled his seat belt. "The phone was too big for my shorts' pockets."

I pulled the car out onto the road and headed home.

"I understand," I said. "I've lost my phone too. I'm really glad they found it, but the consequence is that Daddy has to drive to Orlando tomorrow to pick it up and he didn't plan on spending hours in the car."

The embarrassment of making his youth group wait was heavy on my son's heart, as was his daddy's displeasure. My husband and I dealt out a suitable and appropriate punishment and the subject was dropped.

I won't make fun of him or tease him. He made a mistake and he trusts me to not bring it up over and over. If his brothers try to use it against him, I'll step in. In this small way, I'm continuing to be a safe place for him.

God does the same for us. We sin on the daily, yet Jesus's overwhelmingly beautiful love for us covers that sin. He doesn't throw it in our face. Instead, He allows us to bear the consequences of our actions and then drops it and we move on.

What a gracious God we serve.

What a safe place He is.

Michelle's Intel

I was having lunch with a friend of mine, and we were discussing our children's career paths. Her son and both of my daughters were still in college, but all had declared their majors. Abby was a junior at Indiana University, majoring in early childhood education, and Ally was enrolled at the Fashion Institute of Design & Merchandising in LA, majoring in product development. My friend's son was a ministry major at a small Christian university, but he had just informed her of his plans to go to the mission field.

I looked up from my salad to see her in tears.

"When he told me," she confessed, "I felt like I'd been punched in the gut."

She continued sharing with me all her fears about him pursuing missions, and I listened intently, letting her cry and share. As she was finishing, I heard the Holy Spirit say something I'll never forget, and I knew I was supposed to share it with her.

So I did.

"I don't want this to sound super spiritual or flippant at all, because I can't even imagine how heartbroken and scared you must be, but let me share with you what the Holy Spirit impressed on me just minutes ago: the safest place for your son to be is in the center of God's will for his life, and if that's on the mission field, then you have nothing to worry about."

As soon as I spoke those words, the cloud of fear and doubt lifted, and we were able to continue our lunch.

I've thought about those words many times since that day, and peace overtakes me each time I do. While we can't always be the safe haven for our children, especially as they get older, God *will* always be that safe refuge for them.

As moms, we have to realize that God loves our children even more than we do. So, don't worry—just give your children to God (1 Sam. 1:28). It's the best thing you can do for them.

God Calls Me into the Shelter of His Wings

What a glorious God we serve. Psalm 91:4 says, "He will cover you with his feathers, and under his wings you will find refuge." God offers us safety and protection when we seek Him, the same way that when our kids need us, we kneel down and open our arms to them.

The next time you feel afraid, weary, or frustrated, just remember that God calls us to Him and wraps us in His love so our spirits can find rest.

Prayers of Safety for Your Kids

When we pray for our children, we need to pray for their safety emotionally, physically, and spiritually.

- Emotionally: Father, we trust that You'll protect my children's hearts from embarrassment, cruelty, and teasing. Help them to love others and shield them when others do them harm.
- Physically: Dear God, place legions of angels around my children today. Guide their steps so they will not fall. Keep them safe from harm and invisible to anyone who would dare hurt them.
- Spiritually: Loving and Gracious Father, we know this battle is not against flesh and blood. Please protect my children from spiritual warfare and from all evil that we cannot see. Open my children's hearts to hear Your voice as You guide their steps.

All this we pray in Jesus's name, amen.

44

They Call Me Worrywart

Michelle's Intel

Why didn't they call?

Abby, my then nine-year-old, had gone to a theme park with her best friend. I had felt okay about letting her go—but that was before the tornado warnings had been issued. Now I just wanted her home—crouched in the hall closet with the rest of us. I wanted to know she was safe. I wanted to hug her. Jeff and I prayed that God would watch over her. Still, worry filled my heart. I needed to know she was all right.

Just then, the front door opened.

Abby was home.

In those prior moments of worry, I had heard that still small voice deep inside me saying, "Be still and know that I am God." But I couldn't be still. My mind was filled with scary scenarios and doubts. I wanted to trust God, but this was my baby!

Well, I'd like to tell you I've gotten better at this trusting thing, but when it comes to my daughters, I still struggle. I'd like to tell you that once they're grown and leave the nest, you can finally breathe . . . but I'd be lying. No matter how old they are, they're still your babies, and it's still tough to let go and let God.

In 2016, Abby married her college sweetheart, and though they said they were going to wait five years to start a family, they waited like five minutes. Of course, I was thrilled at the thought of becoming a "Gigi," yet as Abby's pregnancy became more and more problematic, worry started to overtake me. Then, when Abby was diagnosed with preeclampsia at thirty-three weeks, my worries grew. And, when her baby came via an emergency C-section after thirty-four hours of labor—four weeks early— my worries turned into full-on fear. And, when my adorable little grandson was whisked away to the NICU, I was numb. And, when the doctors couldn't get Abby's blood pressure stabilized, I panicked.

I knew her baby was being taken care of by the best NICU team, but *my* baby was still struggling. I had to leave her hospital room for a few minutes because I didn't want her to see me cry. I needed to be strong for her. As tears streamed down my face, that same verse, "Be still and know that I am God," that had ministered to me when Abby was nine, came up strong in my spirit again. True, we were facing a different kind of storm this time, but we served the same God.

Just then, my phone went off. It was a text message from my close friend Eva, who had been a nurse before becoming a writer. I'd been keeping her abreast of the situation, and the last text I'd sent said, "I'm really afraid, Eva. Abby's blood pressure . . . it's not good. And apparently she's losing blood from somewhere. They're giving her blood right now."

To which Eva simply answered, "God's much bigger than that."

She was right, and that's what we had to meditate on as Ab's health and the baby's status changed, sometimes moment by moment, over the next few days.

It wasn't the way any of us had pictured Abby's pregnancy or Baby

Bear's birth, but God proved to be much bigger than all that, just like Eva had said. The end result—as bumpy as that road to recovery was for both my daughter and my sweet grandson—was a healthy, happy Mama Bear and Baby Bear. Praise God!

And the blessings continue.

At the time of writing this, it seems Baby Bear will be a big brother in a few months, and of course, we are all very excited. But I've got to be honest, as soon as I learned the wonderful news, my mind drifted back to all the complications from the last pregnancy and birth. I knew I couldn't dwell in the land of what-ifs, so I said out loud, "No, I'm not going to worry. God is bigger than all of that." I needed to hear myself declare that faith statement because faith comes by hearing, and I've been declaring it every day since.

Often our expectations of how things will go in life are not exactly, or even remotely, how they actually transpire. And, if your faith is easily shaken, those difficult situations can be devastating—especially when they involve your children. Listen, I don't know what you're facing today. Maybe you're experiencing a problematic pregnancy. Or maybe you have a terminally ill child. Or maybe you have a teen who is addicted to drugs.

Life is messy, and at times it can seem too much to carry. But you don't have to carry the load alone. If you're in the middle of some craziness, wondering how you got there and why God is allowing it to happen, quit wondering and start proclaiming: "God is bigger than all of that."

Bethany's JETTliner

So far we've been blessed to have avoided any major surgeries or injuries with our children, although my sweet middle son had bronchitis when he was super little and that was a scary ordeal. Thank you, God, for safety, healing, and protection.

I find that my biggest worry is that I'll fail my kids.

My oldest is almost thirteen, which gives me only five more years—five years—to teach him and raise him before he's off on his own. Five years is nothing. Five years is a finger snap. Five years is a blink.

I can't make the days shorter. I can't freeze time.

There are so many what-ifs that we can drive ourselves crazy with all the possible ways we can fail our children. Did they get enough attention? Did I parent them the way they needed? Was I gone too much? Did I nitpick? Have I smothered them? Did I give them the foundation for life that they needed?

What if I fail them in some way that I can't even recognize?

What if I wasn't enough?

And as the root of the worry rears its hideous head, a small voice whispers into my heart, "God is enough."

God is everything.

I'm definitely going to fail at this parenting thing. I will mess up but God loves my children more than I can fathom (which is difficult to imagine), so I can trust that He isn't going to let me ruin them. God has a plan and purpose for my children and little old me isn't powerful enough to stand in His way.

What we can do as moms is partner with God and ask Him to reveal to us how we can assist in raising these beautiful blessings to be leaders and servants of His kingdom.

We don't have to worry because God is big and He is mighty and He calls us to have peace.

God Calls Me Peaceful

John 14:27 says, "Peace I leave with you; my peace I give you. I do not give to you as the world gives. Do not let your hearts be troubled and do not be afraid." According to this verse, we have been given peace. Let's be honest; it's impossible to have peace and anxiety at the same time, right? Worried thoughts have no place in our lives. Let's practice peace. And remember: no matter what, God is bigger than that.

From Worry to Worship

Now, I'm not saying this is going to be easy, but I am saying it will work. I speak from experience. The next time you start to worry about anything at all, put on some powerful praise music and worship God! You can't worry and worship at the same time.

As you sing about God's faithfulness and His goodness, your worries will crumble in the presence of Almighty God, and praise reminds you every time that He is on the scene. Get your worship on!

45

They Call Me Overprotective

Bethany's JETTliner

One of the hardest parts of parenting your children is letting them learn, and sometimes fail, on their own.

I'm guilty of being an overprotective parent. My first reaction is to say *no* but it's out of fear. I've had to learn to say *yes* even when it scares me, as long as their request isn't too dangerous or crazy. Frankly, sometimes my no was because of a selfish desire: I simply didn't want to have to stop whatever was happening that day to rush a kid to the hospital when he would inevitably fall off the skateboard and break his arm. *Not today, kid.*

This willingness to let go does not come easily, which is why I admire Hannah from the Bible so much. Her story touches all of us in some way, but her ability to give over her son is awe-inspiring. She pleaded with God for a son and promised that if He gave her the desire of her heart, that she would turn her son over to God "for his whole life" (see 1 Samuel 1:27–28).

As soon as her son was weaned, she followed through.

It's hard enough to send my babies to camp or to Grandma's for a week. Handing them over to someone else to raise? Forget about it.

Granted, helicopter parenting, the term used to describe those of us who can't stop hovering over our children for the small basic things, actually causes our kids harm because they don't learn to self-regulate their emotions or take responsibility.

And yes, what is considered dangerous today was totally allowed when I was growing up. For instance, I'm not sure my kids have ever seen a merry-go-round.

The truth is, our kids are going to be hurt in life. Our job is to walk beside them, shield them from the dangerous stuff, yes, but teach them to adapt and handle the situation. People are going to say mean things, kids and adults alike. Truthfully, my heart has never broken the way it does when one of my children gets their feelings hurt. It pains us when our babies are mistreated, left out, or ignored, more so than if we had taken those hurt feelings directly.

God gave us those precious littles to nurture, and with that comes the responsibility of helping our kids overcome adversity . . . and learn from their inevitable stupidity.

If you do a backflip off the swings, you might get hurt.

When someone calls you names, it's okay to be upset. It's how they handle the disappointments and frustrations that will either help them or hurt them as adults.

We must teach our kids coping mechanisms so they don't grow up to be entitled brats as adults. A study from the University of Maryland found that kids who were raised by parents who never let them experience their emotions—that is, they weren't allowed to be sad because their parents would cheer them up immediately—tended to be more depressed. Basically their findings show that strong social and emotional skills are a better indicator of success in college and after high school than reading or writing.[13]

We can teach kids to recognize their feelings and let them know it's okay to have those feelings. If they lash out, we correct that behavior. Journaling is a productive way to work through feelings. Allow your kids to share with you how they feel. You need to be the safe place where they can share those emotions.

My mom taught me and my siblings to be objective by pointing out where we could've done something differently and making us verbalize our thoughts on the other person's perspective. I hated this as a child but this skill of objectivity has helped me immensely as an adult. When my boys fight with their friends over a video game or Pokémon cards, we talk about the bad behavior (name calling, throwing a fit, etc.). If their feelings get hurt, I let them experience it while giving them hugs. Then we talk about it, and if restitution needs to be made on their part, I explain how they need to do that.

It doesn't matter if the other person says they're sorry, but we say it because it's the right thing to do. Teaching our kids that we can't change other people but that we can change ourselves will only help them.

Michelle's Intel

Somewhere deep within all moms lurks "Warrior Mom—Protector of Her Young." And when Warrior Mom surfaces—look out!

I remember one time when my Warrior Mom persona came out to play. I was really sick of this mean-spirited little girl who had been

---

13. Amy Morin, "A 19-Year Study Reveals Kindergarten Students with These 2 Skills Are Twice as Likely to Obtain a College Degree (and They Have Nothing to Do with Reading)," *Inc.*, November 14, 2017, https://www.inc.com/amy-morin/kinder garteners-with-these-two-skills-are-twice-as-likely-to-get-a-college-degree -according-to-a-19-year-study.html.

bullying Abby all year at school, and she had finally crossed the line. The latest incident of bullying had been so ugly and blatant that I was actually shaking with anger. Abby was crying and heartbroken, and I was ready to fight. Warrior Mom was just about ready to call that horrible little girl's mother and give her a piece of my mind. I was going to say something like, "Your daughter is a mean little girl, and I suspect she learned it from you." That was going to be my opening line when I heard the Holy Spirit say: *Giving her a piece of your mind won't bring peace*. Of course, He didn't speak to me in that Morgan Freeman kind of audible voice, just that still, small one.

I longed to verbally annihilate this woman for raising such a bully, but God prompted me to pray for her and her daughter instead. Of course, that was the last thing I wanted to do. Warrior Mom isn't a pray-er, she's a fighter! But I listened and I prayed. Do you know what happened? Abby and that little girl became friends, and later I was given the opportunity to pray with her mother during a family crisis.

If I had acted on my Warrior Mom instincts, I would never have had the opportunity to pray with this family. God didn't need Warrior Mom to handle the situation. He just needed me to follow His leading. The next time Warrior Mom is awakened in you, remember that God's got a better way, and He is your child's ultimate protector.

God Calls Me Safe

In the same way that we protect our children, our heavenly Father protects us. Psalm 91:14 says, "Because he holds fast to me in love, I will deliver him; I will protect him, because he knows my name" (ESV). Even as an adult, it's comforting to know that God has my back and will fight for me and deliver me. No matter how old our kids get, we want them to know that their mama has their back and will fight for them.

Coping Skills for Kids

1. Share your feelings.

2. Journal or draw.

3. Release the energy by running or playing.

4. Listen to calming music.

5. Spend some time alone.

46

They Call Me Late-Night Project Doer

Michelle's Intel

As I hot-glued another rhinestone on the last wrist corsage, I glanced up at the clock.

How could it really be 2:10 in the morning the night before Abby's wedding? And why did I say I'd write all the wedding guest names on the giant chalkboard seating chart?

I already knew the answer. It was the same answer for why I stayed up the entire night of prom all four years, chaperoning After Prom and making breakfast for dozens of kids who ended up crashing at our house. It was the same answer for why I stayed up all night making "Good luck" signs for every football player as part of my cheer mom duties. And it was the same answer for why I stayed up many nights with my girls when they were sad, scared, or sick.

Because I'm a mom.

It's just what we do.

And, though both of my girls are now married and we are empty-nesting, I still find myself pulling all-nighters if either of my daughters needs me. The title of mom is a lifelong one, and I wouldn't have it any other way. I bet you wouldn't either.

But that doesn't mean it's an easy job. Not by a long shot. From the time we find out we're pregnant, that little miracle growing in our bellies keeps us up. From getting up to pee at all hours of the night, to the occasional bout of morning sickness that doesn't just happen in the morning, to excessive heartburn—that little baby starts demanding our attention 24/7.

Yes, every stage involves late nights. When they're infants, we're up feeding them every two to three hours. When they're toddlers, we're often up in the night with a child who won't sleep in his own bed or a child who doesn't feel well. When they're in elementary school, we stay up late working on the map project due tomorrow that you didn't find out about until 10 p.m. Even when they're grown and heading back to college, we stay up until we get that all-important text message telling us they made it safely back to campus.

Late nights, all-nighters, or simply those nights when you can't sleep because you're worrying about your children—they all take their toll. But let's be honest. Though we don't love the late-night projects, we do love that our kids need us. It's a privilege to help our kiddos, even if it means less sleep. So the next time you're up hot-gluing sequins on a spirit stick for cheer camp or sewing patches on your son's Boy Scout uniform or washing your daughter's favorite pair of jeans because she really wants to wear them to school tomorrow, don't grumble your way through the night. Instead, use that time to pray for your children. You're already up, so you might as well put that time to good use. And just know that thousands of moms all over the world are probably up, too, so you might say an extra prayer for your #momtribe.

We're a rare breed. A royal sisterhood. Superheroes in need of a whole lot of concealer. But more than anything, we're the ones our children count on 24/7. So wear those dark circles with pride. You've earned them.

Bethany's JETTliner

If I went to bed early my kids would think I was sick.

They only see me in one mode: Get done tonight what needs to be done for tomorrow. Homeschool portfolio reviews are Tuesday? Never fear. On Monday afternoon we'll be scrambling to assemble notebooks and gluing projects that we started four months ago.

Procrastination is a problem for me, I'll admit, but the main reason I stay up so late (with the dark circles to prove it) is because I'm trying to spend intentional time with my kids every day.

I will not wake up one day when they're grown and gone and regret all the time I spent working instead of playing with them. I caught myself slipping into that black hole of workaholism and I escaped by the grace of God before it was too late.

My plate is overflowing right now. I'm in a long season of hustle but I will not waste moments with my kids.

You might find yourself in this crazy cycle as well but take heart. The emails will be there when the kids are asleep. Clients can wait. You may stay up late and get up early but only do it if it means you're able to get some quality time in with your babies. It's a lesson I'm still learning and teaching myself daily. You've got this.

God Calls Me Able

First Thessalonians 5:24 says, "The one who calls you is faithful, and he will do it." He has called us to this motherhood thing—late-night projects and all—and He is faithful to help us accomplish what we need to do. Oh, that's good news! When we feel we can't do it, God is faithful and will do it through us. And He is right there with you—even when you're burning that midnight oil, baking one hundred cupcakes for the school bake sale. Psalm 121:3 says, "He will not let you stumble; the one who watches over you will not slumber" (NLT). Isn't it comforting to know that when we're up, God's up too? Those promises are even better than Bye Bye Under Eye concealer from IT Cosmetics, and that stuff is amazing!

Wake Up!

Here are a few tips to help you stay awake when caffeine just isn't cutting it and you still have fourteen cheer bows to make.

You're welcome.

1. Keep the right snacks on hand. Eat snacks with a carb-protein combination such as peanut butter crackers.
2. Get some fresh air. Open a nearby window or simply walk outside for a minute or two.
3. Use essential oils or candles. Surround yourself with scents of citrus or peppermint for an immediate burst of energy.
4. Play some upbeat music. For me, it's '80s tunes but whatever gets you going, crank it up to wake up.

During the seasons you need to stay up and help your children, leaving you running on fumes, God will strengthen you and renew you so you can accomplish much! He can cause your four hours of sleep to feel like ten. His touch is way more effective than an energy drink, so put your trust in Him, and praise Him for supernatural energy and renewal.

47

They Call Me Organizer

Bethany's JETTliner

God is not a God of chaos or confusion, but of peace. And a messy home is not a peaceful home.

Sometimes I wish I was obsessive over having a pristine home, and I respect the people who are, but so many times I feel like I'm failing when my house isn't completely organized. First Corinthians 14:40 says all things should be done decently and in order, so when life gets overwhelming, it's time to implement a home management system.

Your home should function for your life instead of trying to make your life work to fit your space. With five of us currently living in a three-bedroom, one-car garage townhouse with one of the worst-designed kitchen layouts ever (only three cupboards?), I'm feeling a bit squeezed. Not only do I work from home, but we've also made the decision to homeschool, so the house has to function for four of us spending the majority of our time within its walls.

1. Declutter and donate. If you haven't read Marie Kondo's incredible

best-selling book, *The Life-Changing Magic of Tidying Up*, I highly recom-
mend you order it pronto. She helped me get rid of items that I'd actually taken the time to protect with Bubble Wrap, items that I *thought*
were precious until I shifted how I thought about my possessions. After
moving several boxes across the country for a military move, I surprised
myself by selling and donating most of the items before we moved again.

Once the house is decluttered, it's time to organize.

2. *Containerize.* Placing items in a container provides boundaries.
The simple act of setting a cake stand beside your sink and adding your
dish soap and sponge to it provides a definite place for these items. Anything that needs to be on the counter can easily be put into a pretty bas-
ket. This tricks the eye into seeing a clean counter.

Organizing "like" items into size-appropriate containers also cuts
down on the time spent searching for things. I created a "scents" box that
holds air freshener refills, plug-ins, wax tarts, and candles. When I need
to replace an air freshener, I know exactly which box to tell my kids to
get. Which brings me to the next point . . .

3. *Delegate.* Part of organizing is keeping the house tidy. I feel like
a great mother when I take care of the laundry and dishes and dusting and vacuuming, but I also have to work, and working from home
means a 24/7 constant pull and guilt. When I work in one area, it's time
away from another. So in the Jett home, we follow a simple system with
a simple question: Do Mommy's hands need to switch the laundry or do
Mommy's hands need to work on the computer *or any adulting chore of
your choice?*

Knowing how to do laundry, dishes, dusting, and vacuuming prepares my children for the day they leave Mama, so teach 'em young!

4. *Maintain.* Perhaps the hardest part of having an organized home
is the maintenance. There are always papers to sort, toys to pick up,
dishes to wash, trash cans to empty, and laundry to put away. Running

a household is not an easy task, and keeping track of meal plans, chore lists, and everyone's schedules is more than a full-time job in and of itself.

A home command center is an easy, customizable solution that offers one location to keep track of the entire household. Ours consists of two dry-erase calendars, one for the current month and one for next month.

Since my boys love to play with dry erase, I use wet-erase markers to prevent important events and deadlines from being erased with one swipe of a grubby little finger. The dry-erase markers cross off the previous day, indicate chores, and let us write notes to one another.

The boys are also using planners this year to organize their activities and chores as well as to manage their time and schoolwork. Their extracurricular activities will continue to grow, so by teaching them to organize their things *and their time*, we're teaching our kids valuable life lessons that will help them well into adulthood.

Michelle's Intel

I am very organized in my writing, but you should see my closet! The truth is, I feel much better about everything in my world if my house is organized. Plus, it saves everyone time because we don't waste minutes searching for the scissors that aren't where they are supposed to be.

Very few things upset my husband. He's a saint, really. But Jeff likes an organized house. He hates it when he looks for the lid to a Tupperware container and none of the seventeen lids in our cabinet fit. That kind of stuff drives him crazy. Knowing that, it's my desire to fix that situation, because I can.

We're moms. We're fixers. We live to serve, right? So even though I'm not uber organized, I am uber in love with my hubby, and I want to keep an organized house for that reason, if for no other. I also wanted to teach my girls how to keep a clean, organized house so when they had their own homes, they could create a wonderful, peaceful, clean, and organized dwelling place.

Just remember that we moms all have different strengths, and we aren't expected to be amazing at everything. I may not be able to organize my cabinets in the best way possible, but I can decorate a porch that will rival any magazine cover. (I learned those decorating skills from my interior-designing sister.) And there will be different seasons where you're better in one area than another, so roll with it. Lead with your strengths and build on your weaknesses. And most importantly, set your children up for future success by teaching them basic skills such as organization. Trust me, they will thank you later, and so will their mates.

God Calls Me Controlled

When we create an organized space, we rid ourselves of unwanted and unneeded clutter, stress, and possessions. We are able to be efficient and ready, and we can model this organization in our behaviors. First Corinthians 14:40 says, "Everything should be done in a fitting and orderly way." Everything. Our actions can become calm and measured instead of reactionary and impulsive, which lets us practice self-control. These are gifts we model to our children, both in our physical caring of our belongings and in the way we treat others.

Create a Home Command Center

Tools

- Dry-erase calendar
- Wet-erase and dry-erase markers

- Place for mail
- Notepad and pens

Find a central location to display your calendar, menu board, mail sorting center, and so forth.

Update the calendar as needed.

Keep the command center free of clutter.

You can find more great ideas by searching Pinterest for "home command center."

48

They Call Me Sentimental

Michelle's Intel

Every morning as I waited in the drop-off line at my daughters' elementary school in Texas, I would take advantage of my captive audience and speak blessings over Abby and Ally. I'd say things like: "God has called you two little girls for such a time as this. And just like Queen Esther, you are going to do big things for God." Other times I'd say, "You girls are walking in the FOG—the Favor of God. Now go have a wonderful day!" And sometimes I'd simply say, "Y'all know how much I love you? Seriously, you are the best part of my day."

As I'd glance back in my rearview mirror, I'd see their sweet little smiling faces, and I'd feel blessed all the way down to my toes. Now, to be honest, as they got older, my words of affirmation were sometimes met with the occasional eye roll, but that didn't stop me because I knew that secretly they liked it, and I also knew they needed to hear it.

I was reminded of this biblical principle of speaking blessings over our children as I began reading *The Forgotten Blessing* by Aaron Fruh, which focuses on Jacob's blessing to his grandsons found in Genesis 48 and Hebrews 11:21: "By faith Jacob, when he was dying, blessed each of Joseph's sons, and worshiped as he leaned on the top of his staff." Basically, Fruh's book emphasizes the importance of the spoken word, specifically the spoken *blessing* over our children.

You see, our children need words of affirmation—especially from those who have authority over their lives—that's us! So, why would we ever withhold those words or miss an opportunity to speak a blessing over them?

Now that my girls are older, I have started writing them "letters of affirmation" for special occasions. I don't do it for every holiday, but I try to write one or two meaningful letters a year, letting them know in writing how proud I am of the women they've become. Sure, I offer an immediate thumbs-up via emoji texting when I learn something exciting—like when Ally was nominated for employee of the month in her design department at Adidas, or when Abby was promoted to interim manager of the preschool where she teaches. But these letters are something more. I really pray over every word, and I include specific examples of how I see God using them to touch the world around them. I encourage them with Scriptures, and I tell them that Daddy and I are cheering them on every single day.

Why have I become so intentional about not only speaking the blessing over my girls but also writing it every chance I get? Because I see the importance of it. When I find a card from my late mother that I've kept in a special drawer or box, I can't wait to open it once again. And, when I reread her edifying words, they still bring encouragement to my heart. Mom's been in heaven more than a decade now, but her words continue to speak to me.

I want to leave that same kind of legacy of blessing for my children, don't you?

I love Christian recording artist John Waller's song, "The Blessing," which reinforces this practice of speaking good things over our children. I encourage you to listen to this entire song during your quiet time with God and really meditate on its message where he asks: *Will we build up? Tear down? The moment of truth is now—this day!*

That really stuck with me—this day. Today. Don't wait to speak blessings over your children. Whether they are babies or having babies of their own, they're never too young or too old to hear your words of blessing.

I can't think of a better time to speak (or write, if you can't deliver the message in person) deliberate words of affirmation over our children than right now. Here's an example of what I wrote to Allyson on her last birthday:

The Top Five Reasons I Think You're Amazing
1. You are a risk taker, unafraid of the what-ifs as you follow God's plan for your life.
2. You are a gifted designer with a very bright future.
3. You have a tender heart, sensitive to God's leading.
4. You possess a quiet confidence that's inspiring to others.
5. You are truly beautiful inside and out!

Of course, you don't have to do a top five list to express your thoughts. Get those creative juices flowing! Maybe you could channel your inner Dr. Seuss and write a fun rhyming poem for your littles. Or maybe you could come up with a word search with all the words to find describing your child. Or you could simply use Scripture to speak over your children. No matter how you package it, the message you share will touch your children's hearts for years to come. You see, by telling our children they are loved by us and their heavenly Father, and by expressing how proud we are of them and the work God is doing in and through them, we give them the best present we could ever bestow—the blessing of affirming words.

That's a priceless gift on any day, at any age.

Bethany's JETTliner

Josiah bounded into my room tonight and chattered about Fortnite, playing with his friend, and how he wished he had a time machine so he could go back and redo a move. I took my hands off my keyboard so I could soak in every minute of his unexpected storytelling. He jumped on the bed and bounced on his knees as he talked.

When he finished, I touched his face and said, "You are such a special kid, do you know that?"

"Yes," he said, and with three bounces he was off the bed and out of the room.

Earlier this evening my middle son Jedidiah gave me a hug for no reason. "You have such a special and compassionate heart, bud," I told him.

He snuggled into me. "Mmm-hmm," he said and I squeezed him tight.

Last night I marked the current day off the calendar and Jeremy teased me for writing the grocery list under the "Ungrounding" heading on our dry-erase board. "I'm glad I'm not grounded," he said.

"You've done a great job at being responsible," I told him.

He smiled. "Yeah, I'm tired of getting into trouble for these little things."

I touched his shoulder and pulled him into a hug. "You're setting a good example and I'm super proud of you."

We praise liberally and often in our house.

"You did a great job cleaning up the kitchen."

"Thanks for folding the towels so nicely."

"I'm proud of you for sharing with your brother."

We're also quick to stifle negative talk and nasty tones. What we say and how we say it are both important. Our house will be a house of positivity. People say cruel things, so I want my kids to have an overflow of affirmation to negate the lies they'll be fed about who they are and what they can become.

Let's not waste an opportunity to edify and build up our children. Let's praise the small acts of kindness and affirm their good behavior. I promise, positivity breeds positivity and our children will thrive as we bless them with the words of our mouths.

God Calls Me to Use My Words Carefully

Proverbs 18:21 says, "The tongue has the power of life and death, and those who love it will eat its fruit." In other words, your words are powerful. With them, you can build up or you can destroy, so use your words wisely. As moms, our words are especially important because our children not only *desire* but also *need* our approval. Let's not be stingy with our praise when it comes to our families.

Build Up Your Children

Practice building up the people in your life this week. Here are a few phrases to get you started:

- You make my life happier just by being in it.
- I love you, and I believe in you.

- You have special qualities others don't have.
- You can do it!
- You are a gift from God!
- I cannot imagine my life without you in it.
- I am so very proud of you.

49

They Call Me Procrastinator

Bethany's JETTliner

When your to-do list is full, it feels like you're always butting up against the deadline.

For instance, I always complete my graduate school assignments minutes before the deadline. No matter how hard I *wish* to get the work done early, a different activity with a shorter deadline takes its place.

Then I read an article about how to ensure you meet your deadlines that changes everything . . . when I implement the advice. #ProcastinateLater

Bryan Harris, owner and founder of Videofruit.org and an email marketing guru, calls it "consequence pricing."[14] The idea is that you give yourself a goal and a time frame, then attach a penalty if you don't succeed. Your penalty has to hurt a little and be enough so you don't dismiss

---

14. Bryan Harris, "Consequence Pricing: 1 Dramatic Change to Improve Your Sales by 15x," Video Fruit, November 4, 2016, https://videofruit.com/blog/consequence-pricing/.

it. So I posted on Facebook that if I don't finish my week's schoolwork by Saturday at 11:59 p.m. Eastern, I'll pay Michelle $100.

A $100 payout would hurt, plus who likes to fail publicly?

However, habits are hard to break, so even though I kept my $100, the assignment was turned in at 11:58 p.m. Eastern on Saturday. I didn't learn a lesson but I did have my Sunday free to be with my family.

My boys inherited this wait-until-the-last-minute disposition. If it takes an hour to do a job, they'll start ten minutes before the deadline. When they inevitably need more time, there is weeping and gnashing of teeth. After I calm down, I lecture them on the importance of starting projects right away.

Unfortunately, my talk doesn't match my walk and they know it.

The Bible encourages a "do it now" instead of "wait till later" approach. "No discipline seems pleasant at the time, but painful," says Hebrews 12:11. "Later on, however, it produces a harvest of righteousness and peace for those who have been trained by it."

I like that the Word says *trained*.

When I see Pinterest-perfect people who are always on time, put together, and completely organized, I die a little. But the Bible says we are trained by the discipline and I don't believe it's a verse about punishment.

Writing daily is a discipline.

Working out is a discipline.

Eating healthy is a discipline *and a punishment when all you want is to stuff your face with chips and chocolate.*

Managing our schedules and learning to say *no* so we can accomplish tasks on time is a discipline.

Ouch. That one hit me right in the gut.

Procrastination is a symptom of poor time management and too many obligations. I'm tired of rushing from one project to the next. By the time I get a little breathing room, I'm already behind on the next project.

It takes less than five minutes to switch a load of laundry but those five minutes multiply if the clothes pile up.

Instead of waiting until tomorrow, let's accomplish our goals now.

We may not be able to do everything on our list but can we succeed in completing three? What if we wrote down three items that need to get done? Two smaller to-dos can have immediate deadlines and the third larger to-do item can be broken down into manageable chunks.

I can't write an entire book in one day, but I can write the rough draft of a chapter.

I can't deep clean my entire home in one day and still accomplish other things, but I can deep clean one room at a time.

Andrew Santella, author of *Soon: An Overdue History of Procrastination*, claims that procrastination gives us a ready-made excuse for poor effort: It's not that I'm not good at my work; I just didn't have enough time.

Interestingly, this self-sabotage is actually called self-handicapping. The researchers who coined this term explain, "By finding or creating impediments that make good performance less likely, the strategist nicely protects his (or her) sense of self-competence."[15]

We need to give ourselves a break, allow ourselves to not be perfect, and create margin in our lives. Our families need us to be at the top of our game. When life feels overwhelming, take a few minutes for yourself, regroup, and tackle the most stressful item on your list. And if you need to implement the consequence pricing, feel free to use me as your payee.

Michelle's Intel

I recently bought a shirt that says, "Running late is my cardio." While that's pretty clever, it's also pretty accurate. I've always had trouble being

---

15. Andrew Santella, "The Real Reason You Procrastinate," *Time*, March 19, 2018, http://time.com/5203895/why-do-we-procrastinate/.

on time. It's not that I want to be late. I even wake up earlier than I need to in order to get ready so that I won't be late. Still, I'm always cutting it way too close, or actually arriving a little late.

But a little late is still late.

Over the years, I've realized my biggest problem is that I try to do too much before I leave the house. For instance, I'll put in a load of laundry or sweep the stairs or rearrange the furniture on a whim—none of which has to be done at that moment in time. Then I end up leaving my house too late to make it to my planned destination on time.

It's a vicious cycle.

While this is aggravating for the people in my life, it was almost crippling for my oldest daughter, Abby, growing up. Like her daddy, Abby feels that being on time is actually being late. She prefers to arrive early, and she's always been that way. It's just how she is wired, so you can imagine the frustration she experienced having me as a mother.

Once I realized how much my lateness stressed her out, I asked God to help me be a better parent to Ab. I asked Him to help me be on time. And He did! I certainly wasn't 100 percent on time every time, but I was a whole lot better, and she was a whole lot happier.

I'm still attaining in this area, but at least I am willing to admit I have a problem. Isn't that the first step to recovery? If you're like me, usually running late, ask God to help you do better. He can, and He will.

God Calls Me Proactive

Scripture is full of examples of proactivity. The teeny ant is praised for her work ethic. She works through the summer so she can enjoy the reward of a long hibernation in the winter: "Go to the ant, O sluggard; consider her ways, and be wise. Without having any chief, officer, or ruler, she prepares her bread in summer and gathers her food in harvest" (Prov.

6:6–8 ESV). There are times to rest, and heaven knows that moms don't take enough time for themselves, but by following the ant's example and proactively preparing for the next stage, the next season, the next semester, we can be more prepared and less tired. Small amounts of time today mean an easier day tomorrow.

How to Stop Procrastinating

- Set alarms and reminders on your phone.
- Set personal deadlines for tasks earlier than the real deadlines.
- Reward yourself for getting projects done early or on time.
- Work in bite-size chunks.
- Schedule work time into your calendar so you don't overcommit.
- Write down the three most important things you have to do for the next day before you go to bed. Complete those three things before tackling anything else on your list.

50

They Call Me Brokenhearted

Michelle's Intel

I pulled into the Best Buy parking lot so Ally could take her iPod in for repairs, but I just couldn't go inside with her. I was still too emotional from her doctor's appointment. I'd been pretty brave throughout her yearlong battle with anorexia, but on that day, I could no longer hold back the tears.

"Mom, I'm trying to get better," she said, sensing my discouragement. "I know you don't think I am, but I don't want to live like this anymore. I want to be better."

Though she'd been in counseling with a doctor who specialized in athletes battling eating disorders, she didn't seem to be improving. She'd gone from a 122-pound power tumbler on the varsity cheer team to an 89-pound skeleton of a girl who wasn't strong enough to even throw a single back handspring. In fact, I hardly recognized that sweet face I loved so much. It was hollow and empty, and I was brokenhearted. I could see we were losing this battle, and I couldn't do anything about it.

Jeff and I had prayed. Her older sister Abby had prayed. Our extended family and friends all over the country had joined us in prayer, but Allyson continued to fade. I wanted Ally to realize she was a precious child of God and that God had a good plan for her life, according to Jeremiah 29:11. But no matter how much I wanted it, I couldn't make it happen. I couldn't make her eat. I couldn't make her well.

Minutes earlier, her doctor suggested we make plans to withdraw Ally from high school at midterm and send her to a facility called Remuda Ranch for intensive treatment. He said he would start the paperwork. I half-heartedly agreed, but I wasn't sure how we would come up with the money since insurance wouldn't cover it. I only knew we had to find a way.

"Mom, I don't want you to be mad at me," Ally said, starting to cry.

"Mad at *you*?" I grabbed her hands in mine and looked her straight in the eyes. "I'm not mad at you. I'm mad at the devil for attacking you like this. I'm mad that I can't do anything about this. And I'm mad that God is allowing it. I'm mad, all right, but I'm not mad at you."

Just then I felt the Holy Spirit nudging me to share Allyson's miracle birth story with her once again, like I had many times before, though I wasn't sure why. I knew Ally knew the story by heart, but the urging was strong so I was obedient.

"Ally, the devil has been trying to destroy you since you were in my womb. That's because you have a big calling on your life. God is going to use you mightily and the devil isn't happy about it.

"You were only eleven weeks old when I started to miscarry you. My doctor sent me home after examining me and said there was nothing they could do. He instructed me to go home and put my feet up, and if I bled a lot more or passed any huge clots, to go directly to the ER.

"When your Aunt Martie heard about my diagnosis, she insisted I go with her to a revival meeting downtown. So, your dad and I went.

"We didn't know that visiting evangelist, and he didn't know us. But when we walked in, he stopped what he was saying, looked at me, and said, 'We've been waiting for you.' We were kind of embarrassed for coming in late, so we sat in the back row. I kept looking down at my belly that wasn't showing yet, praying that you were still in there. Just then, the evangelist stopped the service and said, 'Someone here has been told you are going to miscarry your baby today, and I'm here to tell you that's a lie from the pit of hell. Come up here. I want to pray for you.' I was too nervous to move, and then another lady across the auditorium stood up. He said, 'Ma'am, you're not the one God showed me, but I want to pray for you.'

"Before I could think another thought, the evangelist walked all the way to the back, grabbed my hand, and led me down front. He pointed right at my belly and said, 'I declare today that your little girl will live and not die and declare the works of the Lord!'

"And Ally, the doctor's appointment the next day confirmed what I already knew—I hadn't miscarried. You had a strong heartbeat, and you were born August 15, 1994. Our little miracle."

Ally was sobbing.

"I know, Mom," she said. "I know God has a plan for me."

The presence of the Lord was so strong in the car that day, I could hardly move. We prayed together for what seemed like hours, and when we drove home that afternoon, my broken heart had been restored. Ally was still only eighty-nine pounds, but I knew God was working. I could see it all over her face. A few weeks later, instead of withdrawing her from school, we were celebrating her recovery. I'll never forget Ally's last doctor's appointment that spring. He said, "I wish I could bottle whatever it is that made Ally have such a turnaround."

I just smiled and said, "Well, you can't bottle it but you can access it—it's God."

Every time I share Ally's testimony, or I hear her share it, I am encouraged all over again, but I also know not every story has a happy ending.

If you've lost a baby, or your child has been diagnosed with a serious illness, or your teen has run away from home, I pray peace over you right now. I wish I could reach through these pages and hug you. I want to encourage you to trust God. Let Him love on you and restore your broken heart. He has a way, even when there is no way. He is the mender of broken hearts, and when He puts them back together, they are stronger than before.

Bethany's JETTliner

Loss comes in so many forms. Friends and family have lost babies in miscarriage and stillbirth. They've struggled with infertility and the loss of never experiencing childbirth. We've grieved and mourned together, but that pain runs so deep in their veins that nothing we say or do can ease it.

Dr. Sarah Philpott, author of *Loved Baby*, shares this: "*I need you to know* that you can't take away the pain. Tears will still pour from our eyes and our hearts will still ache. But *I need you to know that we need your love.* Simply showing up means more than you'll ever know."[16]

Romans 12:15 says to rejoice with those who rejoice and mourn with those who mourn. This life is full of pain and sometimes it is unbearable, but God designed you with the mission to comfort others. Support those around you, love them, and walk with them through the heartache and heaviness until their hearts begin to heal again.

---

16. Sarah Philpott, "How to Support a Loved One During Pregnancy Loss," *Loved Baby* (blog), February 29, 2016, http://ourlovedbaby.com/support-loved-one-pregnancy -loss/.

God Calls Me Restored

First Peter 5:10 says, "In his kindness God called you to share in his eternal glory by means of Christ Jesus. So after you have suffered a little while, he will restore, support, and strengthen you, and he will place you on a firm foundation" (NLT).

When our children face serious health battles, it's almost more than a mama's heart can take. We wish we could take away all the pain, and we feel helpless that we can't do anything to change the situation. All we can do is trust God and be there for our kids.

I can't even pretend to know what you are going through if you've lost a child, but God knows, and He understands. His Word says that He will restore, support, and strengthen you and place you on a firm foundation, so stand on those promises today. Remember, you're not alone.

Five Scriptures to Stand On

1. "The LORD is close to the brokenhearted; he rescues those whose spirits are crushed" (Ps. 34:18 NLT).

2. "He heals the brokenhearted and bandages their wounds" (Ps. 147:3 NLT).

3. "Then Jesus said, 'Come to me, all of you who are weary and carry heavy burdens, and I will give you rest. Take my yoke upon you. Let me teach you, because I am humble and gentle at heart, and you will find rest for your souls. For my yoke is easy to bear, and the burden I give you is light'" (Matt. 11:28–30 NLT).

4. "No power in the sky above or in the earth below—indeed, nothing in all creation will ever be able to separate us from the love of God that is revealed in Christ Jesus our Lord" (Rom. 8:39 NLT).

5. "And He said to me, 'My grace is sufficient for you, for My strength is made perfect in weakness.' Therefore most gladly I will rather boast in my infirmities, that the power of Christ may rest upon me" (2 Cor. 12:9 NKJV).

51

They Call Me Patriotic

Bethany's JETTliner

My husband and I love this country and make sacrifices for the welfare of its citizens. The freedom we have isn't free, but until we were back in the military life, I took it for granted.

Now freedom's consequences have names.

Deployment.

Missions.

Security clearance.

Secrets.

Freedom costs me time with my husband. It costs absentee birthdays, holidays, and anniversaries. It costs stress, anxiety, and loneliness.

Yet freedom's reward is beautiful and precious, so we'll gladly make these small sacrifices. My kids will never get back the days their daddy missed while he was gone, but they gained an appreciation for the days that he's here.

Because my husband and I have strong political allegiances, we often discuss our opinions of what's going on in the world. However, it wasn't until our little boys started parroting our comments, particularly about our country's leaders, that I realized I was being slightly hypocritical.

"Say nice things" is a rule at our house . . . unless you're talking about President X.

"Respect authority" . . . unless you don't like the person making the decisions.

This was not okay, so I had to model a more appropriate approach.

"I don't like him" became "I don't like the decision he made," which truthfully allows for a more full-bodied discussion about policy and world affairs.

And while it's perfectly okay to not like or get along with everyone, when my kids would get upset at a friend and say the same words, "I don't like him," I was able to help them transition to "I don't like the decision he made." This keeps the door of potential friendship open and differentiates between a person God loves and a decision the person made.

Respect comes in many forms. My husband always says, "We respect the office even if we don't care for who sits in the seat." And if we can teach this concept to our children early, we are absolutely setting them up to be objective citizens.

This example of teaching respect to our children young was modeled in full force when we were living on off-base housing at an Air Force base.

Retreat played daily at 5:00 p.m. With the first notes sounding from the speaker, a hush fell over the base. Soccer balls were held, kids scrambled out of the swimming pool, and cars stopped moving on the roads.

Service members in uniform came to attention and civilians placed their hands over their hearts. Everyone faced the nearest flag and silently stood out of respect for our country, the flag, the men and women in service, and those who gave their lives.

As the last notes faded away, the statuesque community came to life once more.

Our children didn't need prompting after the first few days, and when the notes played from the speakers, they dropped their toys and stood tall. My eyes always filled with tears of pride and love for my husband and this new journey we were undertaking.

My kids sacrificed for this new life, as well. They left a school they loved, friends they'd grown up with, and a church family they adored. My boys ask every time we move if we're finally going to have our "forever home" and I can't answer with certainty that we will.

We've taught our kids to respect the flag and we're teaching the history of our country. Our kids watched most of the debates during the presidential election and we discussed the issues on both sides of the aisle. They learned about democracy and the electoral system. We teach them how brave our forefathers were when they came to America, and why fighting for freedom is so important.

And when their daddy kisses them goodbye before his deployment, our kids know that his safety isn't certain, but they believe in the reason he's leaving.

We live in a great nation where the majority of our children have access to education, clean water, and food. We aren't oppressed and we can worship freely.

We teach our kids to be respectful of our leaders because we believe that God is in control of nations, and that He alone "deposes kings and raises up others" (Dan. 2:21).

Justin and I have not always agreed with who sits in the president's chair, but what we taught our children is that just like in the military, we respect the position even if we don't care for the person.

We teach our kids to pray for our leaders, asking God to protect them and give them wisdom. We're also guilty of getting a little heated during election season, but it's important that our children understand why our government is so important.

No matter what political positions you hold or which party you claim, let's unite, if just for a moment, as mothers who support one another regardless of our differences. Our diversity makes us great but it is our love for one another that makes us strong.

Being a respecter of persons and a respecter of our leaders is a lesson I want instilled in the hearts of my children forever, no matter the political climate of the day.

Michelle's Intel

It was December 23, and I had just finished signing my children's holiday books as part of the Holiday ICE show at the Gaylord Texan Resort and Convention Center in Grapevine, Texas.

My husband, Jeff, and our oldest daughter, Abby, were with me, along with my cousins Doug and Alex. When we left the DFW Airport hours earlier, the weather in Chicago was cold but clear. However, by the time we arrived in the Windy City, we discovered that a winter storm had beaten us there and blanketed the area with snow and ice. We were thankful we were able to safely land, but as we hurried off the plane and into the terminal, we were greeted with news that all flights had been grounded indefinitely.

We were stranded.

And . . . we weren't the only ones. Hundreds of weary, worried, and angry travelers pushed and shoved their way past us, trying to get the last of the rental cars, while others stared blankly at the overhead screens displaying "canceled" next to every flight.

It was ugly and getting uglier by the minute.

Since it didn't look like any of us were leaving the airport that night, we were given cots. Countless cots and perturbed people—that's what surrounded us. Jeff kept trying to reach our other daughter to let her know the situation, while I tried not to cry at the possibility of spending Christmas Eve and maybe even Christmas in an airport away from my baby girl and the rest of our family.

Just then, my thoughts were interrupted by activity at the gate right in front of us. The last plane of the night had safely landed and the passengers were trickling into the terminal. But these weren't just any passengers. These were soldiers.

It was as if time stood still.

Angry people who had been raising their voices just moments before were silenced by a wave of patriotism spreading throughout the terminal. Suddenly, someone started clapping, then another, and another. Finally, every person joined together and applauded these marvelous men and women in uniform. The tears I had successfully held back began flowing freely as I stood in awe of what was happening. I never wanted to forget that scene: people of all ages and all races, smiling, clapping, and celebrating the selfless soldiers.

Overwhelmed by the impromptu show of respect, the uniformed heroes were literally stopped in their tracks. Some wiped tears from their eyes. Some nodded and thanked the crowd. And some pointed up above as if to humbly say, "All the applause goes to God . . . I'm just doing my job."

That night forever changed me, and it made a big impact on Abby as well. Since then, every time I see a man or woman dressed in uniform, I simply take time to say, "Thanks for serving our country. I appreciate you." I encourage my children to do the same. It's so important to raise our children to love and respect our leaders, and it's vital we teach them to pray for our leaders and our military.

God Calls Me Citizen

As much as I love where I live, it is not my forever home. Philippians 3:20 says, "But our citizenship is in heaven. And we eagerly await a Savior from there, the Lord Jesus Christ." The Bible says that Jesus died, was buried, rose from the dead, and appeared to many before going on to prepare a place for us. As Christians, it is our duty to live for Jesus on earth as we eagerly await the day that He comes back to take us home.

Raising Respectful Kids

- Show respect to the men and women in uniform.
- Pray for our leaders.
- Visit (or learn about online) the historical sites.
- Learn about your country's history—the men and women who have sacrificed for the freedoms we enjoy today.
- Teach your kids to be good citizens to others and to appreciate diversity.
- Share how our freedoms affect you personally.

52

They Still Call Me

Michelle's Intel

"Mom. Mom. Mom. Mom. Mom . . ."

Some days, I wondered if my girls were trying to break a record for how many times they could say "Mom" in a single twenty-four-hour period. On those days, a five-minute potty break alone was the equivalent of a luxury vacation. I relished every moment of solitude because I didn't get very many, or any at all, on most days.

During that season, well-meaning folks would say to me, "Enjoy your sweet babies because these are the best days of your life."

I'd smile and nod my head as the smell of baby spit-up filled my nostrils and a forty-pound diaper bag pained my shoulder.

As time marched on and my babies became toddlers, I'd see those same people at the local Walmart, and they would say the same thing: "Enjoy them while they're young because these are the best days of your life."

I'd force my best fake smile as Allyson rolled on the floor in a terrible twos temper tantrum and Abby pulled over an entire display of stuffed animals.

Then my girls entered preschool and elementary school. And the same people kept saying the same thing, but suddenly I realized my reaction wasn't the same. Knowing my baby days were all in the past, and those cute little toddlers were maturing into adorable, intelligent, funny little girls, gave me the wake-up call I needed.

These really are the best days of my life, I thought.

And I was right . . . sort of.

All the school programs, homeroom mom duties, dance recitals, cheer competitions, proms, homecoming parades, gymnastics meets, back-to-school shopping trips, track-and-field days, talent shows, school plays, choir concerts, senior pictures, college visits—they were all wonderful.

Even the heartbreaks, tutoring sessions, injuries, sibling fights, growing pains, disappointments, breakups, college entry exams—they were still wonderful because those challenges made Abby and Ally stronger, more appreciative of the good times, and more reliant on God.

I'll never forget sitting in the bleachers next to my hubby, watching Abby and Ally cheer together as part of their high school cheer team and wishing I could press Pause on the remote control of life. I loved that day. I loved cheering on my girls as they cheered on their team. I loved rushing home to fix pizza rolls, bagel bites, and chicken wings for our girls and their friends who would crash at our house after the game. Lots of teens, lots of laughter, and lots of love filled our house.

These are the best days of my life, I thought.

And I was right . . . sort of.

Then, it was time for the girls to pursue their own dreams. After leaving Abby and Ally at their respective colleges, we headed home, empty nesters for the first time. It wasn't that I was sad to be alone with Jeff. Even after twenty-two years of marriage, we were still very much in love. I just didn't know who I was or what purpose I would serve without my girls. My favorite job—the one I'd loved for more than two decades—was over. At least that's what I thought when we returned to our house, empty except for the three cats and two dogs that greeted me as I put down my bag.

I wondered if the best days of my life were truly all behind me.

Just then, my cell phone vibrated. It was a text from Ally: "I miss you and Dad already. I know you're sad, but don't be, Mom. We'll still see each other on breaks. I love you so much. You'll always be my best friend." I wiped away the tears just in time to read another text coming through, from my college sophomore, Abby, who had just transferred to a Christian college in Florida: "Hey, Mom, can we Skype tonight? I need some face time with you." It was as if God was letting me know my mom job wasn't over. My girls still needed me.

I loved flying out to LA for some mom-daughter time with Ally, experiencing fashion shows at her design school, and hiking Runyon Canyon together. Jeff and I loved watching Abby perform with her college cheer squad—we were quite the proud parents. And later when Abby transferred to Indiana University and pledged a sorority, I loved going to mom-daughter outings together.

These are the best days of my life, I thought.

And I was right . . . sort of.

Soon after their college graduations, both girls were engaged to the men of their dreams, and I was in full "Mother of the Bride" mode, a role every mama dreams of! The first time I saw both girls in their wedding dresses, they actually took my breath away. My daughters looked like the princesses they'd always been to me. All the planning, shopping, hot gluing, decorating, and stressing birthed two very different, very lovely weddings within the same year. As I watched each daughter dancing with their daddy at their receptions, I was overcome with so much love and pride.

These are the best days of my life, I thought.

And I was right . . . sort of.

After their weddings and honeymoons, Abby and her husband moved three hours south of us, and Ally and her husband moved ninety minutes north. They were all very happy, working in their chosen professions, starting beautiful lives together. Again, I wondered if my official role as mom was over. Would they still need me? Would they still call?

Even if they didn't, I'd come to terms with it; my heart would still be full of all the wonderful memories I had locked away over the years. I remember journaling: "It's really true what they say—the days are long but the years are short. I am so grateful for every moment of it."

Then I received calls I never expected—calls from my babies telling me they were expecting their own babies. First Abby, then Abby again, and now Ally. I will be Gigi to three babies under the age of two by the time this book releases.

In fact, I've just finished helping Abby decorate for and host our grandson's first birthday celebration. Watching Baby Bear dig both hands into his very own cake and grin at me with icing covering his entire face brought this crazy joy to my heart I can't even put into words. I wanted to press Pause once again.

These are the best days of my life, I thought.

And I was right.

I've learned that every stage with our children holds the best days of our lives because here's the truth: they are all "the best days" if you'll view them as such. Enjoy every age! Take it all in! Because life is short. Time passes swiftly. Psalm 90:12 says, "Teach us to realize the brevity of life, so that we may grow in wisdom" (NLT).

Amen. And let me add this, thank God every day for the privilege of being a mother. I promise you'll never tire of hearing, "Moooommmm!"

Although, I'm loving my new title of Gigi maybe even a little more. Just don't tell my girls.

Bethany's JETTliner

When Justin and I went for premarital counseling, our preacher gave us a great piece of wisdom: "This is your party. The kids are only invited."

The meaning was clear. At the end of the day, Justin and I were the ones who committed to "until death do us part." Our children would grow up and leave the nest one day, so we had better make sure we still liked each other.

The thought of my boys leaving home someday breaks my heart. What if they marry girls in far-off places across the country?

What if they don't call me when they're older?

What if they don't come home to visit?

I can't control those situations, so I'd better do my utmost to have an amazing relationship with my boys now . . . while they can't get away!

Additionally, the best thing I can do for my boys is love their daddy . . . and you can bet your bottom dollar that I love Justin Jett more than anyone or anything in the whole world (besides God, of course).

Someday my boys will marry and have kids and start lives of their own. I won't be the main woman in their life. That's how God intended it, so I have to be okay with that. Ephesians 5:31 promises that my sons will leave me: "A man will leave his father and mother and be united to his wife."

If I do my job right as their mommy and teach them and raise them to be godly men, I pray that God will bless my efforts and strengthen my relationship with each one of my boys. I pray that Jeremy, Jedidiah, and Josiah grow up to be men of valor and men of God, and I also pray that

I hold a special place in their hearts so that while they may leave, they won't leave for long.

God Calls Me Blessed

Proverbs 31 is one of my favorite passages in the Bible, especially verse 28: "Her children stand and bless her" (NLT). Okay, let's be clear here, our children may not arise and call us blessed every day, but if we keep raising them according to His Word, that's our promise.

In the busyness of life, it's easy to forget what a great gig we have as moms. It's even easier to forget when your kiddos are fighting in the back seat of a long road trip or your teenage daughter accidentally backs her car through the garage door. Still, "Mom" is a pretty amazing name to be called, so don't take it for granted. Enjoy the motherhood journey, realizing the road is paved with more blessings than you'll be able to post on social media, and that your heavenly Father is leading the way.

Capturing Memories

I'm rarely without my camera or my smartphone, which means I'm always taking pictures. Of course, I'm not a professional, though I had a few photojournalism classes at Indiana University as part of my major. Still, I like to pretend I'm a pro.

There's an amazing photographer just north of where we live named Jeff Richardson (he did my girls' senior pictures, prom pictures, Ally and Wesley's engagement pictures, etc.). When I'm in full-on photographer mode, my family lovingly calls me "JRich," short for Jeff Richardson, lol.

But Abby and Ally and the rest of the family have learned to appease me and let me take photos of every event, every family celebration, and even some everyday shots if the lighting is super good.

Yes, I've totally embarrassed them by whipping out my selfie stick and making the family pose with me on the Vegas Strip or at a Chicago Cubs game, and when I post those pics I'll feature the #sorrynotsorry hashtag because I'm really not sorry. I will never apologize for capturing family memories on my camera or phone. Those photos of the people I cherish most in life are my most priceless treasures.

I bet you feel the same.

If you do, here are three tips for taking the best pictures of your children.

- Take lots of photos: With kids, especially little ones, it's often hard to get a pic with all eyes open and everyone smiling. So take numerous pictures of the same pose to increase your chances of getting a great picture. And be sure that you end up in a shot or two as well.

- Don't miss the candid shots: Sometimes, the best pictures happen while setting up for the next posed shot. If someone says something funny, and the whole family is laughing, snap a photo. Capturing pure joy on film is precious and makes for a wonderful picture.

- Work with the lighting: The golden hour, or sunset, as we nonprofessional photographers call it, usually provides the best lighting. (That's why you'll see so many bride and groom shots being taken outside at sunset.) But if sunset isn't an option, just make sure the light isn't directly behind the subject of the photo, or too much in front of the child, which will cause squinting. Either find a shady place for some quick pics or work around the sunlight. The best portrait lighting is diffused light, so work until you can find that through your lens.

Conclusion

It's been a roller-coaster ride of emotion as we delved into the deeper recesses of our hearts to share the sometimes hard-to-say-out-loud truths that come with motherhood. We've laughed and cried throughout the writing and rewriting of these chapters, and each and every word was chosen carefully and thoughtfully.

We wanted to make sure your voice was heard, so we said the hard things.

We wanted to make sure your feelings were understood, so we put words to emotions that are hard to explain.

We wanted to make sure your thoughts were validated, so we put on our brave girl pants and wrote the thoughts that are hard to express.

You are the role model, the teacher, the risk taker, the boo-boo kisser, the late-night project doer.

You are the most precious person in the entire world to the child who has the privilege to call you Mom.

And you are not alone.

You are part of our #momtribe, and we hope this book is the first step in connecting, sharing, and growing together through this messy, marvelous, mysterious, amazing mom life.

Michelle

Michelle Medlock Adams is an accomplished journalist with over 50 industry awards, an inspirational speaker, a *New York Times* best-selling ghostwriter, and the author of over 90 books. Married to her high school sweetheart, Michelle loves being a Gigi and anything leopard print. Connect with Michelle at www.michellemedlockadams.com.

Bethany

Bethany Jett is a multiple award-winning author, speaker, and business owner. She is a military wife to her college sweetheart and a work-from-home mama of boys who loves suspense novels, cute shoes, and all things girly. Connect with Bethany at bethanyjett.com.

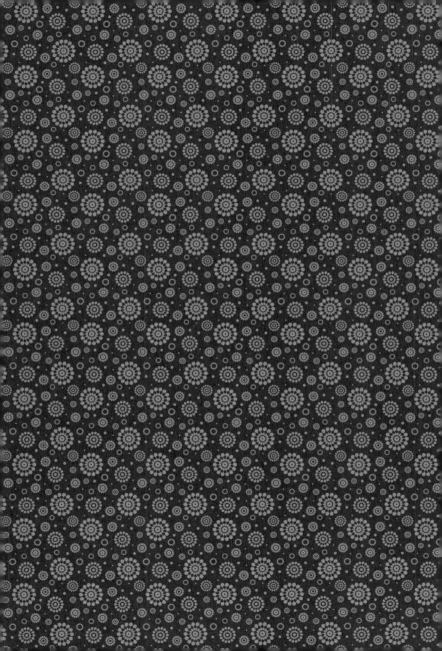